Organizational Discourse

Key Themes in Organizational Communication

Organizational Rhetoric, Charles Conrad
Organizational Discourse, François Cooren
Dissent in Organizations, Jeffrey Kassing
Organizational Socialization, Michael Kramer
Communicating Emotion at Work, Vincent R. Waldron

Organizational Discourse

Communication and Constitution

François Cooren

polity

Copyright © François Cooren 2015

The right of François Cooren to be identified as Author of this Work has been asserted in accordance with the UK Copyright, Designs and Patents Act 1988.

First published in 2015 by Polity Press

Polity Press
65 Bridge Street
Cambridge CB2 1UR, UK

Polity Press
350 Main Street
Malden, MA 02148, USA

ISBN-13: 978-0-7456-5421-8
ISBN-13: 978-0-7456-5422-5(pb)

A catalogue record for this book is available from the British Library.

Library of Congress Cataloging-in-Publication Data

Cooren, François.
  Organizational discourse : communication and constitution / François Cooren.
    pages cm
  Includes bibliographical references and index.
  ISBN 978-0-7456-5421-8 (hardcover : alk. paper) -- ISBN 978-0-7456-5422-5 (pbk. : alk. paper) -- ISBN 0-7456-5421-5 (hardcover : alk. paper) -- ISBN 0-7456-5422-3 (pbk. : alk. paper) 1. Communication in organizations. 2. Organizational behavior. 3. Corporate culture. I. Title.
  HD30.3C658 2014
  302.3'5014--dc23
2014018711

A catalogue record for this book is available from the British Library.

Typeset in 11 on 13pt Sabon by
Servis Filmsetting Ltd, Stockport, Cheshire
Printed and bound in the by Clays Ltd, St Ives PLC

The publisher has used its best endeavours to ensure that the URLs for external websites referred to in this book are correct and active at the time of going to press. However, the publisher has no responsibility for the websites and can make no guarantee that a site will remain live or that the content is or will remain appropriate.

Every effort has been made to trace all copyright holders, but if any have been inadvertently overlooked the publisher will be pleased to include any necessary credits in any subsequent reprint or edition.

For further information on Polity, visit our website:
politybooks.com

À Daniel Robichaud

Les amis, qu'on craint moins de mécontenter que les indifférents, sont toujours les derniers servis

Denis Diderot
Lettre à Madame d'Épinay

Contents

Acknowledgments

I want to express my deepest gratitude to the colleagues and graduate students from our research group, the LOG (Language Organization Governance). These people are, in alphabetic order, Gerald Bartels, Joëlle Basque, Nicolas Bencherki, Chantal Benoit-Barné, Nili Berner, Boris H. J. M. Brummans, Mathieu Chaput, Maurice Charland, Geoffrey Da Costa, Hélène Giroux, Alain Létourneau, Kirstie McAllum, Thomas Martine, Frédérik Matte, Daniel Robichaud, James R. Taylor, Elizabeth E. J. Van Every, and Consuelo Vasquez. A special thank you to Stephanie Fox for greatly improving the readability of the manuscript.

All my love to Nancy, Nina, Émile, and Adrien.

1

What is (Organizational) Discourse?

How is This Book Organized?

Let me begin this book by recalling what will certainly sound like a common-sense truth to many of you: *communication matters in organizations*. We all have already heard this refrain, especially when members start complaining about something that does not appear to work in their company or institution. One department fails to communicate a vital piece of information to another, and a whole project might start falling apart, with sometimes dire consequences (the 1986 space shuttle *Challenger* disaster was partly attributed to a lack of communication between engineers and managers; see Tompkins, 1993).

Communication indeed matters, but as this book will show, it should not be reduced merely to the transfer of information, as is usually implied when people deplore so called "communication problems." Just think about what happens (1) when organizational members are celebrating an important anniversary; (2) when the representatives of a company are signing a contract with a client; or (3) when a supervisor is asking her supervisee to complete a specific task. Are these persons informing each other? Yes, to a certain extent, if we consider, in case 1, that organizational members might be informing each other of their sense of joy and accomplishment; in case 2, that the company representatives are informing their counterparts of their engagement; and in case 3, that the supervisor is informing her supervisee about the kind of work that has to be done.

But if some pieces of information were definitely conveyed

1

(literally, informing means "giving a form," which means that when we are informed about something, we are also *transformed* by what we heard, read, or more generally experienced, i.e., saw, smelled, tasted, or touched), it would be a mistake to *reduce* what is happening in these three cases to a sharing of information. To be convinced, we just need to focus on the *verbs* that are used to depict these three situations: celebrating, signing, and asking. Communicating might have something to do with informing, but it also has a lot to do with many other things that go far beyond the transfer of information: emotions in the case of celebrations, commitment in the case of a signature, power and authority in the case of what is requested.

To highlight this distinction from the "communication as information" reduction, some scholars proposed, during the 1990s, to speak in terms of (organizational) *discourse* rather than in terms of (organizational) communication (Keenoy et al., 1997; Oswick et al., 1997; Iedema and Wodak, 1999; but see also Mumby, 2004). Born from "a growing disillusionment with many of the mainstream theories and methodologies that underpin organizational studies" (Grant et al., 2004: 1), this academic movement – which was, at the outset, UK based, mainly in British business schools – posited that the detailed and systematic study of discourse could be a very innovative and productive path to better understand, analyze, or denounce how organizations function or fail to do so.

We are going to see shortly what is meant by discourse and communication, but before doing so it is important at this point to understand that the writer of these lines has a very broad view of what (organizational) communication means and refers to, which implies that oftentimes in this book, we will speak as much about organizational communication as about organizational discourse. The fact that today many scholars (including organizational communication scholars) tend to use the term "organizational discourse" to insist on the key role that all forms of *communication* play in organizational life implies for me that the term "communication" is, by definition, clearly relevant when speaking about what happens in organizations. What we need to defend, however, is a *very broad conception* of what we mean by communication (see, for instance, Jian, Schmisseur, and Fairhurst, 2008a, b).

Having mentioned this caveat, let us now examine the notions of discourse and communication.

What is Discourse (and, By the Way, What is Communication)?

Although the academic world is full of technical characterizations, I always prefer to start from dictionary definitions when I have to specify or explain the meaning of a word. Why dictionaries? Because they contain, especially when they are sufficiently sophisticated, all the various usages of a term, as well as its history and etymology.

Dictionary definitions

So what are the definitions that we can find for the word "discourse" in the 1995 edition of the *Webster's New Encyclopedic Dictionary*?

Dis·course \'dis-ˌkōrs, -ˌkòrs, dis-'\n I : verbal interchange of ideas : CONVERSATION 2 : formal and orderly and usually extended expression of thought on a\ subject [Late Latin discursus "conversation", from Latin *discurrere* "to run about", from dis- + *currere* "to run"] (p. 287)

We see that two definitions are thus proposed: the more ancient one, which identifies discourse with conversation (when people speak to each other, we can refer to what is happening as a form of discourse entertained by two or more persons), and the more recent one, which identifies discourse with a sort of formal speech or address on a specific topic (as, for instance, when we describe a talk by someone as a discourse on the current situation of our economy).

The etymology mentioned in this definition is also interesting, as it shows that discourse has something to do with *going or moving about from place to place*, which is indeed typical of both conversation and formal speech. When we discourse about a specific topic (whether conversationally or in a formal presentation), we tend to cover its different aspects, which leads us from one idea or question to another. If a discourse can be identified (it has its own unity and coherence, as well as a beginning, a middle, and an end), it is therefore also marked by a certain plurality and heterogeneity.

Discourse vs. discourse

If we now turn to what scholars have been saying about discourse for the past 60 years (the linguist Zellig S. Harris, from the University of Pennsylvania, is usually credited for having coined the term "Discourse Analysis" as early as 1952), we see some interesting overlaps with these dictionary definitions. The sociolinguist Michael Stubbs (1983), for instance, wrote that discourse refers to "naturally occurring connected spoken or written discourse," which, as he says, amounts to saying that discourse is "language above the sentence or above the clause" (p. 1).

Before the 1950s, linguists indeed did tend to focus exclusively on language at or under the sentence level. Although this tendency remains very strong (for instance, Noam Chomsky (1957, 1997), the famous linguist and activist, spent his entire career figuring out the right way to analyze sentences like "John is intelligent" or "John put the book on the shelf"), more and more scholars (not only linguists, but also sociologists, psychologists, anthropologists, and communication scholars) began to realize that discourse also had its own logic and organization and that it was consequently worth studying.

Interestingly, they realized that there were at least two ways to conceive of discourse – two ways that, in many respects, echo the dictionary definitions that we have just discussed. James Paul Gee (1990, 1999), for example, proposed to establish an important distinction between "Discourses," with a capital "D," and "discourse" with a small "d" (see also Alvesson and Kärreman, 2000). To explain what he means by Discourses (with a big "D"), he writes:

4

What is (Organizational) Discourse?

The key to Discourses is "recognition." If you put language, action, interaction, values, beliefs, symbols, objects, tools and places together in such a way that others recognize you as a particular type of who (identity) engaged in a particular of what (activity) here and now, then you have pulled off a Discourse (and thereby continued it through history, if only for a while longer). Whatever you have done must be similar enough to other performances to be recognizable. However, if it is different enough from what has gone before, but still recognizable, it can simultaneously change and transform Discourses. If it is not recognizable, then you're not "in" the Discourse. (Gee, 1999: 18)

As Gee notices, when you identify a Discourse with a big "D," it means that you are able to recognize its *typical* form or content (what he calls the *what*), as well as its *typical* context of production (*who* said it and in *what circumstances*).

Think, for instance, of the typical Discourse of a doctor, manager, professor, environmental activist, or right-wing politician and you will have an idea of what a Discourse might look like. It does not have to be in the context of a formal speech (you can easily recognize how doctors typically speak during a simple consultation, or how someone speaks "like a teacher," sometimes even outside the classroom), but what is crucial is that you are able to *recognize* or *identify* something you think you already heard, read, or know.

As we will see later, this type of Discourse analysis is usually associated with the work of the French philosopher Michel Foucault (1977a, b, 1978), who became world renowned for his contribution to the study of the *typical* discursive forms associated with specific historical periods of time and disciplines (medicine, education, justice, etc.). At this point, it is also noteworthy that people who are reproducing specific Discourses can literally be seen as their *carriers*, which means that we could almost say that not only are these persons expressing themselves when they are talking, but also the (typical) Discourses they represent. In this connection, Gee (1999) has no hesitation in writing that:

It is sometimes helpful to think about social and political issues as if it is not just us humans who are talking and interacting with each other,

5

but rather, the Discourses we represent and enact, and for which we are "carriers." The Discourses we enact existed before each of us came on the scene and most of them will exist long after we have left the scene. Discourses, through our words and deeds, carry on conversations with each other through history, and, in doing so, form human history. (p. 18)

This is what happens when we witness two types of Discourses confronting and/or responding to each other. Think, for instance, of the typical Discourse of union representatives responding to the typical Discourse of top managers and you will have an idea of what Gee means here.

So what is a *small "d" discourse* in comparison? It is "language-in-use or stretches of language (like conversation and stories)" (Gee, 1999: 17). In other words, we more or less find here the other dictionary definition, which identifies discourse with "a verbal interchange of ideas," a practice associated with conversation (although we will see that discourse (even with a small "d") cannot be reduced to the mere "interchange of ideas," which sounds like the "interchange of information," which we criticized earlier).

Beyond the identification of typical formats, contents, styles, and contexts (associated, as we saw, with Discourses), studying discourse (with a small "d") thus requires that we analyze the *interactional event* in itself, with its complexity, but also its peculiarities. By this, I mean that however typical, emblematic, representative, or characteristic what someone said or wrote might be, it will always be an *event* in itself, to the extent that the activity of saying or writing what she said or wrote will just have happened *once* in the whole history of the universe.

Although this might sound a little (too) philosophical, it is important to understand this point, to the extent that this whole book will be (directly or indirectly) addressing it throughout the remaining chapters. Discourse analysts can indeed be divided into two broad categories:

1. Scholars who tend to be mainly interested in Discourses with a big "D" and who focus on the repetition, reproduction, or

iteration of specific topics of discussion, styles of communication, and rights to speak. These scholars are, as mentioned earlier, usually associated with Foucault's work, although not exclusively, and tend to be interested, as we will see, in questions of power, ideologies, and domination.

2. Scholars who tend to focus on the eventful character of conversation and interaction, i.e., what we also call discourse (with a small "d") and who are more interested in what people are up to when they communicate with each other (what they do and how they do what they do), as well as how the conversation itself functions and is organized. These latter will usually be associated with the work of Harvey Sacks (1992), an American sociologist who, in the 1960s, founded a field of study called "conversation analysis."

Conversation analysts, as we will see, are typically interested in the detail of what they call "naturally occurring interactions" and focus their attention on what is *done* or *accomplished* by the people who communicate with each other. Although they too are also interested in repetition and reproduction (after all, any scientific endeavor aims at the recognition of patterns), they will usually not go as far as speaking of "carriers" of specific discourses when referring to people in conversation. For them, people engaged in conversations are, first and foremost, developing sensible and meaningful forms of conduct that are produced and recognized as such (Pomerantz and Fehr, 1997, 2011).

We will go back to these two forms of discourse analysis later in this chapter, but at this point, it is worth noting that this distinction between Discourse and discourse has not inhibited other scholars from acknowledging both aspects at the same time in their analyses (see, for instance, Fairclough, 1992; Wetherell, 1998; Taylor and Van Every, 2000, or, more recently, Cooren et al., 2007).[1] In other words, analyzing what someone is saying or writing as a Discourse, that is, as representative of a *typical* way of thinking or speaking about a given topic or question, does not mean that one cannot *also* analyze what she is saying or writing in

7

terms of what she is accomplishing or *up to* in the context of the interaction she is engaged in.

Discourse and communication

Another question that can be raised about discourse in general (whether "big D" or "small d") is related to what *counts* or *does not count* as discourse. Although, so far, we have seen that discourse could be conceived of in terms of its repetitive or eventful character, one could also wonder whether discourse should be reduced to (the product of) verbal exchanges or written documents. Some scholars, for example, consider that the term "discourse" should not only encompass what is said in a given conversation, but also include gestures, intonations, facial expressions, or the proxemic[2] features of an interaction. In other words, they consider all these dimensions to be potentially meaningful in any interaction and that as such they should be included in what we mean by discourse (Jaworski and Coupland, 1999).

Why does it seem so important to extend discourse to its so-called "non-verbal aspects"? Precisely because they are meaningful and they actively participate in (or contribute to) what is performed or accomplished, especially when people happen to speak to each other.[3] Just imagine a boss who would say to her employee, "George, I'd like to speak with you, please," with a big smile and a cheerful tone or, on the contrary, with an embarrassed face and tone, and you will have a pretty clear idea of what this smile and cheerful tone or her embarrassed face and tone are *communicating* to George (and to us), as well as their significance in both situations.

In the case of the big smile and the cheerful tone, chances are that George will be anticipating some good news from his boss ("Will I have some kind of promotion or salary increase?"), while in the other case, he can already anticipate that his world might be falling apart ("Is she about to announce that I am fired?" or "Is our project terminated?"). As conversation analysts like to remind us, everything is potentially meaningful at each moment of an interaction, an idea that they express by using the expression "No time out" (Garfinkel, 2002). "No time out" means that participants engaged in a conversation cannot escape the communication game they are involved in, which means that everything they say, express, or do (consciously or unconsciously) is available for interpretation by their interlocutors (and the analysts).

To this picture we could add, of course, all the things that potentially communicate something in a given situation. Not only is it body language (facial expressions, gestures, postures, etc.), but also *anything* that might make a difference in the way a situation is interpreted: pieces of furniture, decorations, clothes, architectural elements, and so on. This is where the notion of discourse might, to some, no longer look relevant, but where the term "communication" still appears to work. What I mean is that some could question that we identify pieces of furniture, decorations (a painting, for example), clothes, or architectural elements with discourse to the extent that we seem suddenly remote from what people are doing or up to in a conversation.

However, we could also point out that all these things are *telling* us or *communicating* something. To understand this point, think, for instance, about the amount of money that some corporations and institutions regularly invest in the design of their buildings and furniture. Even if these investments might officially have been made in the name of efficiency and comfort, they will also *communicate something* to the visitors and to the employees themselves: majesty, prestige, wealth, modernity, coolness, sobriety, austerity, and so on. All these impressions will be associated with the institution or corporation and will communicate something about them (Kuhn and Burk, 2014).

As proposed by Cooren, Bencherki, Chaput, and Vásquez (forthcoming), communication should thus be generally defined as the establishment of a link, connection, or relationship through something (see also Cooren, 2000). This thing can be as diverse as a piece of information, a feeling of joy or anger, an order or promise, an apology or congratulations. Furthermore, who or what communicates can certainly be individuals, but also architectural elements, artifacts, documents, and even principles, ideas or values (Cooren, 2010). Finally, this link can be established through something that is said, but also something that is written, or even, more generally, expressed (through gestures, facial expressions, or intonations, for instance).

But whether we think that what we try to analyze is more a matter of communication than discourse does not really make a difference, since everything depends on what we end up meaning by our use of these terms (for some discussion, see Jian, Schmisseur, and Fairhurst, 2008a, b; Kärreman and Alvesson, 2008; Putnam, 2008; Taylor, 2008). What does matter is that we start to understand why discourse and communication might indeed represent key aspects of our organizational life.

What is Organizational Discourse?

Having started to explore what the term "discourse" means per se, we can now turn to a second question, which gets closer to the theme of this book: what is *organizational* discourse?

Common sense vs. constitutive definitions

At first sight, an obvious way to define what organizational discourse is would be to say that it is the discourse that is taking place within an organization and/or that deals with organizational issues, whatever they may be (strategies, culture, control, ideologies, coercion, etc.). Studying organizational discourse would thus consist of studying how people are talking, writing, or more generally interacting regarding organizational matters, whether these matters concern, for instance, strategic issues (Vaara and Whittington, 2012) or routine operations (Feldman, 2000; Feldman and Pentland, 2005).

In their *Handbook of Organizational Discourse*, Grant et al. (2004) venture a definition when they write that:

> The term "organizational discourse" refers to the structured collection of texts embodied in the practices of talking and writing (as well as a wide variety of visual representations and cultural artifacts) that bring

organizationally related objects into being as these texts are produced, disseminated and consumed. (p. 3)

Interestingly, we find here the two dimensions of discourse that were highlighted in our previous section on discourse: (1) Discourse (with a big "D") as a "structured collection of texts," which marks the fact that organizational members are reproducing certain Discourses when communicating with each other; and (2) discourse (with a small "d") when they note that these structured collection of texts are "embodied in the practices of talking and writing," which refers to the eventful character of language-in-use.

Note also that they extend the term "organizational discourse" to "a wide variety of visual representations and cultural artifacts" (p. 3), thus echoing our point about discourse as corresponding to anything that is telling us or communicating something, whether it is a document, a turn of talk, a graph, or a piece of furniture.

But what is key in this definition is that these discourses (with a big "D" or small "d") *"bring organizationally related objects into being as these texts are produced, disseminated and consumed"* (p. 3; my italics). For a discourse to be considered *organizational*, according to Grant et al. (2004), we therefore need to go beyond the fact that it is simply taking place within an organization or addressing organizational matters. This discourse also should be considered as *constituting* what they call "organizationally related objects." To understand what they mean here, just think of anything that characterizes the organizational world: official statements, directives, memos, newsletters, annual reports, organizational charts, and so on.

All these "objects" are not only produced, disseminated, and consumed, but also constituted or brought into being by discourse (whether big "D" or small "d"). To this list, we could also add other things that are not, properly speaking, disseminated or consumed, but that also define, in many respects, the organizational world. I am thinking of meetings (Boden, 1994; Cooren, 2007), press conferences (Bhatia, 2006), coordinated activities (Cooren and Fairhurst, 2004), organizational culture (Eisenberg and Riley, 2001) or leadership (Fairhurst, 2007; Fairhurst and Uhl-Bien,

2012). Without discourse, these things would not exist, which means that studying (organizational) discourse becomes a way to understand how things as various as leadership, meetings, or press conferences not only work (or fail to), but also *exist*.

Discourse and organizational constitution

As we now begin to understand, studying organizational discourse does not only consist of analyzing the documents and conversations as well as visual representations and cultural artifacts that compose the events and routines of organizational life, but also amounts, in its strongest version, to claiming that discourse (or communication in general) constitutes the very means by which organizational forms exist or, to put it in academic terms, are *brought into being* (Grant et al., 2004; Hardy et al., 2004). This position is called a *constitutive* approach, and was coined the CCO perspective (for *communicative constitution of organization*) by McPhee and Zaug (2000) as well as Putnam and Nicotera (2009). According to this viewpoint, studying discourse allows us to unveil the mechanisms by which "human beings coordinate actions, create relationships, and maintain organizations" (Putnam, Nicotera, and McPhee, 2009: 1).

Claiming that organizations are discursively or communicatively constituted thus not only means that interactions take place or that documents are circulated *in* organizations, but that, in many respects, *there would not be any organization at all without them* (Ashcraft, Kuhn, and Cooren, 2009; Cheney, Christensen, Conrad, and Lair, 2004; Fairhurst and Putnam, 2004; Phillips, Lawrence, and Hardy, 2004; Taylor, 1988, 1993; Taylor and Van Every, 2000, 2011, 2014). Just imagine what an organization would be without the contracts that are signed in its name, the recurring conversations about its present situation or future, the directives that define what members should or should not be doing, or the mission statements that defines its *raison d'être*? I do not think it is extremely controversial to answer that indeed *there would not be any organization at all*, since it is hard to imagine what an organization would do or be without them.

12

If correct, such a *constitutive* approach to discourse, which has been implicitly defended by some organizational communication scholars for more than 25 years (Taylor, 1988, 1993; Taylor, Cooren, Giroux, and Robichaud, 1996), shows that the role of discourse in organizational settings is far from being anecdotal and that studying organizational discourse gives us access to some of the most basic aspects of organizational life. In this book, I will thus take it for granted that anybody who is interested in organizational discourse will, in one way or another, defend a constitutive approach.

This does not mean, of course, that everybody interested in organizational discourse agrees about the level of constitution (we will go back to this question later, but see, for example, Fairclough, 2005, or Reed, 2010). However, I believe that anybody who takes the question of organizational discourse seriously will admit that this object has some constitutive power, which in turn means that studying it allows us to understand the mode of being and functioning (or dysfunctioning) of organizational forms, whether it is to simply analyze them or to denounce them.

Objectives and Organization of This Book

In order to demonstrate the importance of studying discourse and communication, this book will show how classical organizational themes, objects, and questions can be illuminated from a discursive perspective. Having presented in this chapter, in general terms, what can be meant by (organizational) discourse, I will introduce you, in chapter 2, to *six* ways of analyzing it. The decision to retain only six approaches (semiotics, rhetoric, speech act theory, conversation analysis/ethnomethodology, narrative analysis, and critical discourse analysis) has, of course, its share of arbitrariness. I believe, however, that it is a selection that provides an introduction, rather exhaustively, to the various methodologies and perspectives that have been mobilized during the past 25 years by the growing literature on organizational discourse.

Having done that, I will then show how we can study

coordination and organizing (chapter 3), organizational culture and identity (chapter 4), and negotiation, decision-making, and conflicts in the context of meetings (chapter 5). The choice of focusing on these traditional organizational "objects" or "themes" is, of course, deliberate, as I believe you will be more interested in learning about what these discursive perspectives have to teach you about culture, negotiation, or conflicts than you will be inclined to focus on the various perspectives or approaches that discourse analysis has to offer (there are plenty of readers or edited volumes that already do that: see, for example, van Dijk, 1997a, b; Jaworski and Coupland, 1999).

It is, of course, crucial that you be introduced to the various ways and methods of analyzing (organizational) discourse and how to mobilize them (and chapter 2 is precisely meant to introduce you to this diversity), but I believe it will be more interesting and productive to operationalize these methods, theories, and approaches throughout the book, allowing you to see what these various discursive perspectives can teach us about organizational life in general.

This book will thus be privileging the Indian "blind men and an elephant" approach. What do I mean? According to this ancient tale, a group of blind men is gathered around an elephant, with each of them permitted to touch only one body part of the animal. Having done so, they are then asked to compare their respective experiences, which leads them to realize that they cannot reach an agreement about what it is they have come into contact with. In the Buddhist version of this tale, the man who touched the elephant's head says that it feels like a pot, the one who touched the ear says that it is actually a winnowing basket, while others declare that "it is a plowshare (tusk), a plow (trunk), a granary (body), a pillar (foot), a mortar (back), a pestle (tail) or a brush (tip of the tail)" (Wikipedia, 2014).

You have only to replace "elephant" with "organizational discourse," and you will see, throughout this book, that different scholars tend to privilege different aspects of this specific activity, which leads them to reach different conclusions about what organizational discourse might be, as well as its constitutive role

14

in organizational life.[4] Each chapter (from chapters 3 to 5) will thus correspond to a specific organizational topic or practice (the elephant, in the Indian tale) that will be addressed and analyzed from the six perspectives (the blind men) that are presented in chapter 2. My objective will be to *articulate* these various perspectives without losing sight of their respective specificities.

Throughout the book, the unifying thread will be the communicative constitutive approach (CCO), as implicitly or explicitly advocated by the great majority of organizational discourse analysts and theorists. This unifying thread will also allow me to maintain a global coherence that will help you distinguish between discursive perspectives and other approaches to organizational life.

2

Analyzing Organizational Discourse

Six Perspectives

Let us now turn our attention to the blind men. As mentioned in the previous chapter, I decided to select six of them – that is, six perspectives that will be introduced, discussed, and applied in each of the remaining chapters of the book. These perspectives are: (1) semiotics; (2) rhetoric; (3) speech act theory; (4) conversation analysis/ethnomethodology; (5) narrative analysis; and (6) critical discourse analysis. Other perspectives could have been selected, of course, but the advantage of these perspectives is that (1) they are all well established; (2) they each promote (implicitly or explicitly) a constitutive view of organizational discourse; and (3) although they are focused on discourse, they are broad enough to include other approaches like gender studies (Ashcraft, 2004), deconstruction (Kilduff and Kelemen, 2004), dialogic perspectives (Gergen, Gergen, and Barrett, 2004).

Although my goal is to highlight what is specific to each of these approaches, I will also show what they have in common with each other, especially with regard to their explicit or implicit positions vis-à-vis the constitutive dimension of discourse and communication. In other words, whenever possible, I will demonstrate what each of these perspectives has to say about the constitutive power of discourse and communication vis-à-vis organizational forms.

Semiotics

Semiotics (also sometimes called semiology) has two historical roots: one in Europe, around the work of the Swiss linguist
Ferdinand de Saussure (1857–1913), and one in the United States,
with the philosophy of Charles Sanders Peirce (1839–1914), who
was not only a philosopher but also a logician, mathematician,
and scientist (Taylor and Van Every, 2011). Although this short
presentation will not do justice to the complexity of this field of
study, semiotics can be globally summarized as the systematic
study of signs and their functioning. Saussure (1959) envisioned
semiology as this "science that studies the life of signs within
society" (p. 16) when he noticed that linguistic signs (i.e., words)
were only one type of signs among many others. As for the term
"semiotics," which was proposed by Peirce, it was first coined by
the British philosopher John Locke (1959/1690) from the Greek
word *semeion*, which means a mark, sign, or token.

What makes a semiotic study specific with regard to other perspectives and how does it analyze discourse? One specific trait that
characterizes this approach is that it tends to be first and foremost
interested in the *functioning of signs*, whatever they are, which
means that discourse, for a semiotician, should be understood as
made of signs. What is a sign? A quick answer would be, paraphrasing Peirce, that it is *anything that stands for something else in
some capacity*. A classical example is a series of symptoms, which
could be identified as the signs of a specific disease by a physician. These symptoms (and this is why they could be associated
with a form of discourse) *tell* the physician that the patient she is
observing might be suffering from a given illness, a reading that is
made possible because the physician learned how to recognize the
various signs of this disease.

There are, of course, many different types of signs, which
were all the topic of numerous classifications and typologies
(see Nöth, 1995). For instance, Peirce proposes no less than ten
classes of signs, which he identifies according to what constitutes
for him the three components of any given sign: its *representamen* (the material dimension of the sign itself), its *object* (what

the representamen stands for) and its *interpretant* (what allows the connection between the representamen and its object). In our example, the material aspect of a series of symptoms is the representamen (for instance, a fever, a runny nose, a sore throat, and a cough), the disease itself is the object (for instance, a bad cold), and the physical connection between the disease and the symptoms is the interpretant (the fact that bad colds tend to come with these specific symptoms, as any physician knows).

But beyond this (legitimate) interest in the classification of signs (for more detail, see, for instance, Eco, 1979), what makes the semiotic perspective crucial to anyone interested in discourse analysis is that this approach focuses on how signs come to *do something* in specific circumstances (Cooren, 2008). In other words, semiotics is implicitly interested in the *performative* aspects of discourse itself, that is, what discursive elements do or perform in certain conditions. To illustrate this point, just imagine that you are entering a corporate building and you want to get to a specific location: the office of a law firm, for example. Chances are that you will be successfully directed to your final destination by a series of signs that will lead you there.

For instance, a board posted on the left wall of the lobby will provide you with the list of companies located in this building. Having found the name of the law firm in this list, you will then look at the floor number that the board indicates for this company: 15. You will then get to the elevator and press the call button with the number 15 printed on it, an action that will bring you (hopefully!) to the corresponding floor. Once you've arrived at the fifteenth floor, you will then follow a series of arrows that will lead you to the entrance of the law firm and its recognizable logo. You will then enter the office space, speak with the front desk and sit in the waiting room. Having a chance to look around you (the furniture, the paintings on the walls, the carpets, the way people dress), you will then start to have a general feeling about the type of firm you might be dealing with (conservative, hip, modern, classic, wealthy, etc.).

As we see in this illustration, signs are not simply things that we look at and interpret, they are also – and this point is crucial for a semiotic reading of the situation – *active* or *acting*, that is, they are *doing things*. Peirce called "semiosis" this activity or action of the signs, which you can find in the following series of descriptions.

- The entrance directory *provides* you with the list of the companies and the floor numbers.
- The call button 15 *stands for* the fifteenth floor of this building.
- The arrows *lead* you to your final destination.
- The company logo *confirms* that you now are at the entrance of the firm.
- The way the office space is furnished and decorated *informs* you about the type of company you might be dealing with.

Of course, you could point out that all these signs (the board, the call button, the arrows, the logo, the various elements of the office space) do not do these things by themselves. They need to be interpreted or deciphered by someone (in this case, you, as the visitor). Semiotics does not deny such evidence, but points out that these interpretations precisely consist of *recognizing what signs are doing* (Cooren, 2010; Cooren and Bencherki, 2010; Cooren and Matte, 2010).

For instance, we already saw that someone (usually a physician) has to *know* how to read a series of symptoms in order to recognize what they *tell* him, that is, that the patient is suffering from such and such disease. The same thing can be said about the law firm example to the extent that you have, of course, to be capable of reading or interpreting signs in order to recognize what they do or perform: it is because you know how to read and interpret a directory board, a call button, an arrow, a logo, and even an office space, that you are able to recognize what they are *telling* you. The board is telling you where you should go to get to the law firm; the call button is telling you where you should press in order to get to the fifteenth floor; the arrows are telling you where you should go once you leave the elevator; the company logo is telling you that you arrived at your destination

As we see, semiotics defends (implicitly or explicitly) a very broad conception of communication and discourse. A sign can be a word, a sentence, or even an argument, what Peirce defines as *symbols*, but also an image, an arrow, a footprint, or even a color. For example, a photograph, a painting or an image is a sign, more precisely what Peirce calls an *icon*, to the extent that you are able to recognize or interpret what the image itself (the representamen, in Peircian semiotics) stands for (for example, your cousin Willy, i.e., the object). This recognition is made possible because the image you see on the print *looks like* the Willy you know and who happens to be your cousin. This relation of *resemblance* is what allows you to interpret what the picture does (for instance, this picture *shows* my cousin Willy when he was young), which is what Peirce calls the interpretant. Icons are therefore characterized by this relation of resemblance between the representamen and the object.

Peirce also identifies what he calls *indexes*, which are characterized by a relation of *causality* between the object and the representamen. The example I gave you before about the symptoms is a good illustration of what an index consists of. It is because the disease (the object) usually produces (or causes) these symptoms (the representamen) that the doctor is able to recognize that you must have a bad cold. Footprints and weathervanes function according to the same logic: the footprints indicate that someone walked there and in what direction, and the weathervane indicates the direction of the wind. What is crucial to understand at this point is that a sign can combine several aspects: for instance, an arrow posted on the wall has an iconic aspect (it looks like an arrow and can be recognized as such), but also an indexical dimension to the extent that this arrow *indicates* what path you should follow.

Iconic and indexical dimensions can also be recognized in symbols like onomatopoeias (e.g., words like "bang," "murmur," "ouch!," which have a relation of resemblance with what they refer to, i.e., their objects) or even sentences and arguments. For example, if I say, "This is such an old house!" Peirce would say that this sentence has an indexical dimension to the extent that the demonstrative "This" is used to *indicate* a house I am looking at or pointing to. It also has an iconic dimension in that I am implicitly classifying this house I am looking at or pointing to in the category of the very old houses, a category where houses *resemble* each other with regard to the question of their age. Finally, it has a symbolic dimension to the extent that the six words that compose this sentence (and that are all representamens) have an arbitrary or conventional relation with the objects they refer to (for instance, in French, we would have said *Cette maison est tellement vieille!*).

Again, my point is not to present exhaustively what semiotics is all about (we have only focused on Peircian semiotics so far and this is just a very short introduction at that!), but to show you what semiotics tells us about organizational discourse, especially from a *constitutive* viewpoint. As we saw with the law firm example, a key aspect of the organization of the building space comes from the various signs that are displayed in this locale. Without the directory posted on the wall, the numbers on the call buttons of the elevators, the arrows on the walls, and even the logos at the entrance of the companies, most visitors would indeed be completely lost in this building.

In many respects, signs thus have a constitutive role in organizations and organizing because there could scarcely be any organizational forms without them. This, of course, does not mean that people are passively following what signs are telling them to do (we already show, on the contrary, how active and competent people have to be in order to read signs, i.e., how to understand their law, their *interpretant* – their systematicity). However, it means, as we will see later, that signs play a key role in the structuring and organizing of collective forms. Another way to put it is that signs display a form of *agency*, that is, as we already pointed out, they literally *do things* and it is precisely because we know that they are doing things that we mobilize them so much in organizational settings.

Rhetoric

Rhetoric, as a field of study, has a very old tradition, which can be traced back to the ancient Greek sophists (Corax of Syracuse, Gorgias, Protagoras of Abdera, etc.) who, from the fifth century

BC, defined themselves as teachers of wisdom or specialists of knowledge. In addition to being considered foreigners (most of them were not born in Athens and were itinerant professors), they asked to be paid for their services and claimed they could teach wisdom or even virtue, three factors that contributed to their bad reputation among Athenians, especially two philosophers, Socrates and Plato, who were their intellectual enemies (Foss et al., 1985).

Because of this unfortunate reputation, today, "sophism" is a pejorative word, referring to a fallacious argument or reasoning that is used for deceiving someone. Similarly, rhetoric tends to have a negative connotation in ordinary language as it is often associated with empty words that are claimed to have no connection whatsoever with reality ("This is just rhetoric!" is an expression we often hear, which usually means "These are just empty words!" or "This is bombast!"). Defined by Aristotle (384 BC–322 BC) as "the faculty of discovering in any particular case all the available means of persuasion" and by Quintilian (*c.*35– *c.*100) as "the art of speaking well," or, more recently by Robert T. Craig (1999), as "the practical art of discourse" (p. 135), rhetoric has indeed always been criticized for creating a disconnect between language use, on the one hand, and truth or reality, on the other hand.

Despite these negative connotations, this body of knowledge did more than survive throughout the centuries, through such brilliant representatives as Cicero (106 BC–43 BC), St Augustine (354– 430), Erasmus (1466–1536), or Giambattista Vico (1668–1774), among many others. All were interested, in one way or another, in what could be called the *power of words* or their capacity to *make a difference* in specific situations. Although it came under fierce attack during the modern era (an era that is often associated with the rise of scientific inquiry, first in Europe and, later on, in North America), it has been somewhat rehabilitated during the second part of the twentieth century with the resurgence of interest in the study of language (especially in departments of linguistics, communication studies, and literature).

Two tendencies can roughly be identified in rhetorical studies:

on the one hand, scholars such as Roland Barthes (1988), who tend to restrict the field of rhetoric to the study of the formal aspects of language use (the identification of tropes or figures of speech, like metaphors, metonymies, litotes or allegories) and, on the other hand, scholars such as Kenneth Burke (1945/1962, 1969) or Chaim Perelman (1982, 1984), who broaden the focus to the performative or even constitutive dimensions of language, especially in terms of persuasion and argumentation. Tropes and figures of speech are also objects of study for this second movement, but they are then analyzed in terms of what difference they *make* in the definition of a given situation.

I will concentrate on this second trend, given its connections with the constitutive view of organizational discourse that this book proposes to explore. What is crucial to understand is that rhetoricians tend to be mainly interested in the textual and/or oratorical dimensions of discourse. This means that they will often focus on specific texts or documents as well as on specific public discourses or speeches in their analyses. Although they can be interested in the non-verbal aspects of communication and discourse (for example, Aristotle and later Cicero both insisted on the important role elocution plays in the delivery of a speech), they will tend to privilege the analysis of Discourse (with a big D), that is, the analysis of *a* specific discourse, whether this discourse is taken from a formal speech, an annual report, or a website.

So what is the specificity of a rhetorical approach to discourse, especially in terms of constitution? As mentioned earlier, rhetoric is first and foremost concerned with the power of words, that is, their capacity to make a difference in a specific context.[1] For instance, rhetoricians note that a discourse always *defines a situation* (Perelman and Olbrechts-Tyteca, 1969) and that the choice of words is, of course, the key to influencing how an audience will perceive and understand it. Just imagine a controversial situation where a corporation is faced with accusations of environmental malfeasance. Chances are that the representatives of this corporation, whether through press conferences or official press releases, will define the situation in such a way that their own responsibility is attenuated or even that they should not be held accountable.

Defining a situation is therefore just another way to speak about constitution to the extent that an environmental disaster will be *constituted* as much by the actual effects pollution might have on a given ecosystem (e.g., the number of animals or plants that are contaminated or killed by the disaster, the level of pollution that can be detected in a river or a landfill, the number of particles that will be revealed in the atmosphere, etc.) as by what will be *said* or *written* about it (how they will be characterized, named, or defined, even to the point of negating their existence). The issue, of course, is that what is considered a fact has to be presented and interpreted, which means that the nuance between what pertains to factuality and what pertains to discourse tends to be not that easy to identify and pinpoint.

Interestingly, we find here the old debate between sophists and philosophers, which today sometimes takes the form of a debate between rhetoricians and scientists. While rhetoricians would say that the situation is primarily defined by what is said and written about it, scientists (whether biologists, physicians, engineers, etc.) would respond that the situation should actually be principally defined by the *facts* that are revealed about it, facts that they claim to be able to disclose and represent, faithfully and rigorously. To the power of words that rhetoric puts forward, science thus typically responds with the power of facts and truth.

To reconcile these two perspectives, we could observe that both are, to some extent, right (which is, of course, another way to say that both are, to some extent, wrong!). Bruno Latour (1987) proposes, as a form of response to this debate, to distinguish between a *weaker* and a *stronger* form of rhetoric. As he points out, the definition of a situation will, of course, always depend on the way people come to talk and write about it (rhetoric is therefore safe!), but some versions of this situation will end up looking stronger than others depending on *what* or *who* is made to speak (a position that demonstrates the important role science might play in a debate before the point of deciding what its result might be).

To return to our previous example, the *strength*, *weight*, *power*, or *authority* of any discourse or position officially held by the corporation about their responsibility vis-à-vis a disaster will depend on the number and quality of the *arguments* and *actors* that they are able to mobilize. For instance, they will probably muster engineers and scientists, who will couch the facts in terms that attenuate the corporation's responsibility. In response, opponents will mobilize their own engineers, scientists, and environmentalists to arrive at conclusions that will accuse the company. Whether we like it or not, making the "facts speak for themselves" is therefore a contentious activity, which can lead to never-ending debates between experts, specialists, and so-called "spin doctors."

As this example illustrates, rhetoric does not in and of itself question the existence of facts and factuality; it merely points out that facts always have to be interpreted and communicated in one way or another, something that even scientists do not question.[2] In other words, the meaning of facts will always depend on how they are *made to show and say things* in a given debate. Rhetoricians will also point out that facts are just one type of argument, as people not only debate about the nature of reality, but also about values, norms, principles, and rules, especially how they are prioritized (Perelman and Olbrechts-Tyteca, 1969). In our example, even though the company might not end up denying the fact that they polluted a given area, they still might question the level of compensation they are supposed to give to the population, based on existing laws, what they consider to be their level of responsibility and how they interpret them (i.e., how they make the laws speak).

A rhetorical approach to (organizational) discourse thus consists of being aware that any speech, any text, will define a situation in a specific way and that this definition will, of course, serve specific interests or ideologies to the detriment of others. Following Burke (1945/1962) and McGee (1975), Maurice Charland (1987, 1990) proposes, for instance, the notion of "constitutive rhetoric" when he notes that a specific discourse will always function as a form of *staging* where specific subjects and situations are constituted, usually through the forms of storytelling and narrative. We will go back to this in our section on narrative analysis, but at this point, we should remember that rhetoric focuses on how a specific discourse comes to stage what *matters*, what *counts* in a specific situation, whether in terms of facts, values, or principles.

Speech Act Theory

Speech act theory, as we know it today, was first proposed by a British philosopher, John Langshaw Austin (1911–60), who was curious about the functioning of ordinary language. In his William James Lectures, which he gave in 1955 at Harvard, he started his series of talks by pointing out that language is not reducible to the simple assertion of facts (such as "The cat is on the mat" or "The present king of France is bald"), as philosophers tended to think at that time, a reduction that he proposed to call the descriptive fallacy. Language, in fact, can be used to perform many different things, which he illustrated through several examples: getting married (when, for instance, you pronounce "I do" in the course of a marriage ceremony), promising something (as when you say "I'll be there tomorrow"), or asking someone to do something for you (as in "Could you please pass me that file?").

Although this idea might appear obvious enough, on first reading, it has since been recognized as a revolution in the way we approach and understand the functioning of language. Austin decided to call statements of the type "This is a very old house" or "You look pale" constative (*constater* in French means "to notice" or "to observe"), and the other types of utterances that he had just started to identify (e.g., "I promise to be there," "I order you to come," "I apologize for hurting your feelings," etc.) *performative*. He also stipulated that performative utterances have to be performed by the *right persons* with the *right words* in the *right circumstances* in order to be considered happy or successful.

As a matter of illustration, just imagine the (certainly weird) situation where an unauthorized individual instead of the minister or official who was supposed to pronounce these words suddenly says, toward the end of a wedding ceremony, "I declare you husband and wife." Austin (1962) would call this unexpected declaration unhappy or infelicitous, that is, null and void. The participants would thus have to redo at least a part of the wedding ceremony. Other examples would be cases where the right words would not be pronounced (this is, for instance, what happened to the Chief Justice when he did not pronounce the exact words that Barack Obama was, according to the procedure, supposed to repeat after him for the presidential oath of office, a failure that forced both of them to retake it, see Cooren and Matte, 2010), or where the circumstances would not be the right ones (if, say, someone bet on a horse that turns out to not be running).

All these examples point to the fact that *we do things with words*,[3] and sometimes very important things at that (getting married, hiring or firing someone, becoming the president of the United States, signing an important contract, buying a house, etc.), which explains why certain verbal deeds tend to be *controlled* by who is authorized to perform them, what is supposed to be said and in what circumstances (Bourdieu, 1991). Interestingly, even less formal situations (where there is, for instance, no formal procedure to be followed) can lead to questions of authority and the right to say certain things.

Imagine, for instance, someone who abruptly tells you to "Come here!" instead of the more gentle and polite "Could you please come here?" and you will understand why the right circumstances, the right person, and the right words can have significance in less formal occasions. Although "Come here!" could be appropriate in some circumstances, in others, it could be considered rude and you would certainly be well within your rights to react by saying, "Who are you to be talking to me that way?" (a reaction that amounts to questioning the person's authority or right to speak to you in such manner).

But Austin did not end his reflections here and even began to somewhat purposefully contradict himself in his fifth lecture. The distinction between constatives and performatives was not that easy to defend, since even constatives, as he noted, happen to have a performative dimension. Indeed, when you are noticing, reporting, or stating something during a conversation (which is what a constative is supposed to be all about), you are actually *doing or performing something*: precisely, noticing, reporting, or stating. Furthermore, when you say, "This is a very old house!" (the example of constative I used earlier), you are not only making an observation, reporting a fact, or noticing something (which already are three performatives), but you might also be doing a lot of other things, depending on the context of the interaction and how it is spoken.

For example, you could be marking or expressing your disappointment (if just as you happen to arrive at the property and discover the state of the house that a real estate agent is showing you), your words could be meant and heard as an implicit critique addressed to your interlocutor (something like, "I asked you to show me only new houses and look at what you are showing me!"). Or imagine that you are now the real estate agent and you are speaking to your client before getting to the house. Then "This is a very old house!" could be meant and heard as a warning, marking an attempt on your part to prepare your client for what she is about to see (or alternatively as an attempt that could also be meant and heard as a mark of attentiveness, on your part, to your client's needs).

As these illustrations make clear, people are doing or performing many different things with language: they not only say what they say ("This is a very old house!"), but they can also insinuate, imply, convey, or suggest many things *in saying* what they say ("I am disappointed," "You are an incompetent real estate agent," "I am warning you that this house might, at first sight, disappoint you," etc.). By highlighting the performative aspects of *any* utterance (including what he initially called "constatives"), Austin thus paved the way to a vast program of research that spread well beyond philosophy and began to influence fields as varied as linguistics (especially what is today known as pragmatics, i.e., the study of language use, see Levinson, 1983), communication (Cooren, 2000), and organizational studies (Ford and Ford, 1995).

One of his former students, the American philosopher John R. Searle, later took up Austin's reflections and developed his own version of speech act theory (many others exist – see, for instance, Habermas, 1984). In a well-known classification (Searle, 1979), he identified five types of speech acts, which he named *assertives* (e.g., "You look pale"), *commissives* (e.g., "I'll be there tomorrow"), *directives* (e.g., "Give me that file, please"), *declarations* ("I declare this session opened"), and *expressives* ("I apologize for the inconvenience"). In order to differentiate between these different types of speech act, he suggested that they could be classified according to their *direction of fit*.

Assertions, as he noted, are characterized by a *word-to-world* direction of fit. For instance, "You look pale!" is an assertive (what Austin initially called a constative) in that the words pronounced are supposed to fit with or adjust to an independent state of affairs (the world), i.e., the fact that you indeed look pale. He further claimed that directives and commissives are, on the contrary, marked by a *world-to-word* direction of fit, that is, this time, it is the world that is supposed to fit with or adjust to the words. Commissives like "I'll be there tomorrow" have a world-to-word direction of fit because it is by being present tomorrow at a specific location that you will make the world fit with your words, that is, what you just said.

Similarly, directives like "Give me that file, please" also have a world-to-word direction of fit. By actually giving you the file that you are requesting, your interlocutor is supposed to transform the world in such a way that it fits your words. What distinguishes commissives from directives is that in the case of commissives, *you*, as the speaker, are the one who is supposed to transform the world so that it ends up fitting with your own words. In other words, you are committed by your own words, that is, your words commit you to do something. In the case of directives, however, it is your interlocutor who is supposed to enact this transformation, that is, he is the one who is supposed to be committed by your words.

Searle then noticed that a fourth category exists, that of declarations, which are marked by a double direction of fit (both word-to-world and world-to-word). For instance, when a chairperson says, "I declare this session opened" at the beginning of a meeting, she is not simply stating something (the fact that the session is now opened), she is actually opening the session by pronouncing these very words! We can speak of a double direction of fit because it is almost as though a declaration consisted of claiming the existence of something that is, in fact, created or produced by the very fact of declaring it.

In comparison with other types of speech act, declarations are actually the ones that seem to express the most performative aspects of language. When an authorized person declares, in the appropriate circumstances, "I hereby declare you husband and wife," "The court pronounces you guilty of murder," "We approve this decision," transformations take place that have important consequences: people are now considered married, guilty, or they see their decision approved. And note that someone can be considered guilty without even committing any crime, a point that shows, again, the constitutive power of discourse.

Finally, Searle identified a last category of speech act, the expressives, which are characterized by a null or empty direction of fit. For instance, when you say, "I apologize for the inconvenience," you are, according to Searle, expressing an apology about something that already took place and caused some inconvenience for your interlocutor. You are not claiming or reporting that something happened (it is not an assertive) or committing you or your interlocutor to do something (it is not a commissive or directive), but you are certainly doing something important: acknowledging a fault and presenting your excuse, which can be accepted or not by your interlocutor. Furthermore, you are also underscoring your relationship with your interlocutor and, in this way, redressing the wrong in the past in order to have better relations in the future.

While rhetoric insists on the capacity of words to *define* situations, speech act theory shows that words can go beyond the activity of definition, to the point where they also participate in the very *transformation* of situations. Furthermore, we will see later that speech acts can be considered the building blocks by which organizing takes place (Cooren, 2000; Taylor, 1993), which, of course, means this approach clearly demonstrates how organization and organizing are *communicatively constituted*.

Ethnomethodology/Conversation Analysis

In many respects, ethnomethodology and conversation analysis both echo the tenets of speech act theory, even if, to my knowledge, their representatives were never directly influenced by Austin's (1962) and Searle's (1969, 1979) writings. This lack of influence can be explained by the type of questions that ethnomethodologists and conversation analysts are interested in, questions that are quite different from the ones that speech act theorists are asking. In order to illustrate these parallels and differences, let us see where ethnomethodology and conversation analysis come from, what they mean, and what their questions (and responses) are.

Ethnomethodology literally means the study of the methods (*methodo-*) people (*ethno-*) mobilize in their daily life to generate social order. It is the sociologist Harold Garfinkel (1917–2011) who first coined this word when he noticed that the jury members he was observing in a Californian court of law during the 1950s were putting into play specific methods, procedures, and techniques in order to go about their business as jurors, even if they had never served as jurors before. More importantly, he noticed that these methods, procedures, and techniques were, in many respects, enacting or producing a specific order (e.g., electing a foreman, trying to reach consensus, rendering a verdict, etc.), which is typical of how juries function (Garfinkel, 1967). What does it mean concretely? Simply that studying the detail of any social activity can give us important clues about how people in interaction construct or even constitute the very situation they are involved in.

Although Garfinkel's (1967, 2002) ideas are certainly hard to grasp (but see Heritage, 1984, as well as Livingston, 1987, for excellent introductions), his way of conceiving of the origin of social order revolutionized sociology from the 1960s, a revolution that later came to pervade other fields as varied as communication, management studies, and linguistics. In order to fully grasp what this revolution consists of, let us examine a very simple social fact we are all familiar with: formatted queues or service lines (Livingston, 1987). As we know, formatted queues or service lines pervade our world: they tend to form as people are collectively waiting to be served by a clerk, whether it is in a bank, in an administrative office, or at the entrance of a stadium (just to name a few examples).

As Garfinkel (1967, 2002) noticed, formatted queues have, like any social fact, a paradoxical nature. They have a specific mode of existence – that is, they can be identified, distinguished, and recognized as such, but this mode of existence depends on how the queues are interactively enacted by the people who participate in their production. Of course, without the people who are forming a queue, it seems obvious there would not be any queue at all, but Garfinkel goes one step further in his reflection by noticing that the participants are not passively forming a service line, but are *actively* producing it by orienting and reacting to various aspects *they know* constitute what a formatted queue is supposed to be about.

In order to illustrate what Garfinkel means here, just imagine a person who, as we say, *butts into the line*, that is, someone who (willingly or unwillingly) bypasses the queue by directly going to the counter in order to be served. Chances are that the people who form the queue will complain about this type of behavior and that someone (a person who is waiting in the queue or one of the clerks) might even intervene in order to tell the intruder that he has to do like the others do, i.e., wait for his turn. Even if this point looks, at first sight, trivial, it is actually crucial and can be explained more fully by a key term that Garfinkel introduces, which is the notion of *accountability*.

What does accountability mean? It means that any social situation, any action, any decision, is a priori considered to be both intelligible and assessable. For instance, in the formatted queue example, we saw that someone who butts into the line immediately becomes the object of critiques and could even be asked to *account for* his deviant behavior. "Butting into the line" is accountable to the extent that it is something all participants not only recognize, identify, make sense of, or distinguish (it is an intelligible conduct), but also deplore, condemn, criticize, or denounce (it can be sanctioned). There are therefore ways (methods or procedures) to be in and to compose a line-up, as well as ways (methods or procedure) to intervene if something does not work as expected.

Furthermore, and this is a crucial point in Garfinkel's reasoning, it is this accountable character of any situation that, in many respects, maintains a normative order. There are things you *can* and *should do* and things that you *cannot* and *should not do* when you form or join a formatted queue, but Garfinkel shows that it is *the participants themselves* who actively orient to these questions and concretely deal with them in their conduct. A formatted queue is accountable because people *know* what it is supposed to look like and how it is supposed to work, which presupposes that every participant will adopt specific methods or conducts (not being too far from or close to each other, moving forward when it is time to do so, etc.) that are meant to be recognizable, identifiable, accountable as appropriate, normal or suitable. The very existence of the queue thus depends on its accountability, that is, the fact that it is intelligible, reckonable, observable, reportable, comprehensible, evaluable or assessable.

Another key notion that Garfinkel proposes is *reflexivity*, which is directly related to the issue of accountability. It is noteworthy that by using this terminology, Garfinkel does *not* mean to refer to people's capacity to reflect on their own experience. What he means is that *what people do* and *say* in a given situation actively participates in the definition, production, and even constitution of that very situation. Reflexivity literally means the state of what is in relation to itself, as you might remember from your math courses (for instance, the relation "is equal to" is a reflexive relation). Going back to the formatted queue example, we can notice that people's conduct is not something that only happens *in* a context (for instance, in a bank, in an administrative office, or at the entrance of a stadium). It also defines many aspects of this context, such as the very fact that people are waiting in line in order to be served.

This notion of reflexivity is crucial to understanding the *constitutive* dimension of discourse and communication, as it refers to the fact that when people interact with each other, they reflexively produce important aspects of the context or situation. Using another example, we could notice that when a boss is speaking to her supervisee, she is not only doing that *in* a given context or situation (her office, for example), but she is also, in speaking in a certain way, *producing* or *constituting* many dimensions of this context. For instance, if what she says sounds dictatorial and imperious or, on the contrary, convivial and friendly, her conduct will reflexively enact not only a specific relationship (cold vs. warm), but also specific identities (e.g., an authoritarian vs. collegial boss).

Garfinkel notices that people in interaction constantly *orient* to these accountable and reflexive characters of conduct. This means that participants are the ones who actually negotiate and identify what is happening in a given situation. For example, what looks like a dictatorial or imperious conduct on the supervisor's part could actually be considered perfectly normal and even acceptable by the supervisee, an interpretation on his part that would be illustrated by his compliance and absence of negative reactions. Ethnomethodologists thus do not take any definition of a given situation for granted, but on the contrary rely on what people say and do to see how this situation is negotiated or confirmed by the participants. This position distinguishes them from speech act theorists who tend to identify speech acts without relying on how participants orient to what is said or done.

Garfinkel thus observes that people are not "judgmental dopes," an expression that means that we, as analysts, should rely on how people *produce* and *make sense* of a given situation in order to define what the situation basically is. In other words, defining a situation as, for instance, confrontational or collegial is not something that only the analyst does. Defining it also and especially relies on how people make sense of and enact this very situation. Garfinkel thus proposes a sort of Copernican revolution in social sciences as he puts forward what could be called a *performative* vision of society (Latour, 2005). According to ethnomethodology, it is, first and foremost, the people in interaction who constantly negotiate, define, and produce the world in which they evolve, whether it is a given context, a group, an organization, or a society.

Several scholars were influenced by Garfinkel's approach,

among them Harvey Sacks (1935–75), who developed a sister discipline called conversation analysis. What characterizes conversation analysts is that they always work from the audio or video recording of naturally occurring interactions, an approach that sets them apart from speech act theorists who tend to only focus on invented cases (see Levinson, 1983). Although conversation analysts are mainly interested in mundane conversations, they can also study institutional interactions (e.g., classroom interactions), as well as situations where no specific words are pronounced (e.g., individuals waiting to be served in a store). What thus interests them, in general, is the functioning and organization of interaction, without being restricted to conversations per se.

Extending the tenets of ethnomethodology, conversation analysis thus "treats the conduct of everyday life as sensible, as meaningful, and as produced to be such" (Pomerantz and Fehr, 1997: 69). This means that conversation analysts tend to analyze not just what people are *up to* in a given interaction – that is, what they are trying to achieve and how they manage to do this – but also what they are reacting or responding to and how they are doing so. It is also assumed that "meaningful conduct is produced and understood based on shared procedures and methods" (p. 69), which implies that, in order to interact, people rely on some sort of mutual knowledge, which allows them to recognize and understand each other's conduct.

Finally, conversation analysis highlights the *sequential* aspect of discourse and interaction. Any turn of talk (or speech act, for that matter) can be understood and analyzed as *responding* or *reacting* to a current context (what was just said or written before by someone else, for instance), but also as *renewing and transforming* this context, by the very fact of responding/reacting to it. Conversation analysts thus invite us always to analyze what is said or written as *depending* on its context of production, even if they also highlight what people are doing in saying or writing something that will, by definition, transform or modify this context. As we saw in the section on speech act theory, what "This is a very old house" means (informing, warning, complaining, criticizing, etc.) depends on the context that this utterance or turn of talk is responding to, but also on how it is then treated and understood by the interlocutors.

Another characteristic of this approach to discourse is that conversation analysts try to transcribe the detail of interactions as faithfully as possible. They will usually work from transcripts, that is, written versions of a discussion that took place verbally. Of course, in the case of written interactions, for example, online discussions, there is no need to transcribe since the original material is already in a written form. In most cases, the lines of the transcript are numbered so that it is easier for readers to locate the turns of talk that are analyzed.

Conversation analysts, especially Gail Jefferson (1984), also developed conventions to integrate information about gestures, intonations, pronunciations, overlapping, and so on. In what follows, I summarize some of these conventions with the excerpt of a transcript taken from a conversation between two managers, Denis and Helena. These conventions will be extensively used in the rest of the book, so it is important that you understand them well:

138	Denis:	I wish [I was there].
139	Helena	[It's such a] great place to live
140	Denis:	Meanwhile he is so:: annoying=
141	Helena	=Yes, but so gentle with us
142	Denis:	In any case (.) you know
143	Helena:	It's too late
144		(1.5)
145	Denis	Yep, definitely
146	Helena:	Anyway
147		((Helena's cellphone rings))
148	Denis:	Okay, so see you in fi- uh I mean three days
149	Helena:	Yes, no problem >see you soon, Denis<
150		(1.0)
151	Helena	Hello, Nancy?

As you notice, each line of the transcript is numbered, including the line where there is a 1.5 second pause in the discussion (line

144). Here is an explanation of the various conventions I used to create this transcript:

- Brackets [ ] indicate that the encased portions of the utterances are produced simultaneously. Left-hand brackets designate the beginning of simultaneity, whereas right-hand bracket mark its end.

  138   Denis: I wish [I was there].

  139   Helena   [It's such a] great place to live

  On lines 138–9, Denis and Helena respectively say "I was there" and "It's such a" at the same time.

- Colons :: indicate the extension of the preceding sound.

  140   Denis: Meanwhile he is so:: annoying=

  On line 140, the colons indicate that Denis lengthens the pronunciation of the word "so."

- Equal signs (=) indicate that there is no time elapsed between two utterances.

  140   Denis: Meanwhile he is so:: annoying=

  141   Helena   =Yes, but so gentle with us

  When Denis finishes his turn of talk with "annoying" (line 140), Helena immediately starts her turn by saying, "Yes" (line 141). There is no interval between the two turns.

- Period in parentheses (.) indicates a very short pause (less than one tenth of a second).

  142   Denis: In any case (.) you know

  The pause between "case" and "you know" on line 142 is almost imperceptible but noticeable.

- Numbers in parentheses – e.g. (1.5) – indicate intervals in the stream of talk (here, 1.5 seconds). These intervals (indicated in seconds and tenth of seconds) can be identified within an utterance or between utterances.

  143   Helena: It's too late

  144   (1.5)

  145   Denis   Yep, definitely

  (1.5) indicates that 1.5 seconds elapse between the completion of Helena's turn and the beginning of Denis's turn.

- Double parentheses (( )) indicate that what is encased is a description of what is happening during the interaction. What is enclosed is not a transcription.

146   Helena: Anyway
147   ((Helena's cellphone rings))

On line 147 ((Helena's cellphone rings)) indicates something that is happening just after Helena said "Anyway" on line 146.

• Hyphens - indicate that the prior syllable was cut off short.

148   Denis: Okay, so see you in fi– uh I mean three days

Denis is about to say "five" but stops and rephrases what he means to say.

• The signs > < indicate that the words pronounced between them are produced with a higher pace than the rest of the talk. The signs < > indicate that the words pronounced between them are produced with a lower pace.

149   Helena: Yes, no problem >see you soon, Denis<

Helena says, "see you soon, Denis" with a higher pace than "Yes, no problem."

I could dedicate many more pages explaining the ins and outs of conversation analysis and ethnomethodology (for more details, see Boden, 1994; Hutchby and Wooffitt, 2008; Pomerantz and Fehr, 1997, 2011; Silverman, 1998), especially regarding how the previous excerpt could be analyzed. However, I think that the best way to understand this perspective is to actually analyze sequences of interaction, which is what we will do in the remaining chapters.

What is key to our comprehension at this point is that conversation analysis and ethnomethodology invite us to study discourse in terms of *meaningful and accountable actions* that people perform in their daily conduct. Furthermore, it is these actions that come to define, produce, and constitute the situations in which people evolve, a principle that Garfinkel identifies as the *reflexive* dimension of our conducts (see also Boden, 1994). Finally, representatives of this perspective focus on the *embodied* or *incarnated* character of discourse, which highlights its situated dimension, that is, the fact that a given discourse or turn of talk always responds to specific issues and concerns, which people are concretely dealing with.[4]

Narrative Analysis

With speech act theory and conversation analysis, we have just seen that sequential or longitudinal aspects of discourse are crucial to understanding what is going on in a given context, that is, what *constitutes* it. With narrative analysis (i.e., the study of narratives and narrative structures), we are now addressing a perspective that also focuses on this important dimension, especially through a reflection on how people collectively or individually create, report, or make sense of the evolving aspects of a situation.

As several scholars note (Barthes, 1977; Bruner, 1991; Czarniawska, 1997b; Taylor and Van Every, 2000), storytelling is a very common and mundane activity, which is not restricted to the writing of novels or the telling of tales. People indeed tell stories all the time, whether it is to recount what happened at a party the day before, report on some activities or events that are taking place in an organization, or tell a joke that will simply lighten the atmosphere during a meeting. Some even speak of a narrative construction of reality (e. g., Bruner, 1991; Fisher, 1984, 1985; Czarniawska and Gagliardi, 2003), which implies that narratives are not transparently telling us what an independent reality might actually look like. They are constructing or constituting it.

Narratives indeed consist, as we will see, in *selecting, naming,* or even *inventing* aspects of a given situation or sequence, aspects that are meant to serve the purpose of the storytelling or the storyteller's interests (impressing, denouncing, praising, arguing for a specific position, etc.). As we all know, stories are indeed often characterized by their *moral,* which corresponds to what we are supposed to retain or learn from them, that is, what their *uptake* or meaning is or should be. People thus are not only telling stories or recounting events, they are also accomplishing various things in doing so: convincing or discouraging someone, building a specific case, or simply making conversation by trying to say something interesting (this is why, by the way, some conversation analysts are interested in storytelling, e.g. Lerner, 1992).

It becomes clear that narratives thus have their own logic, so to speak, and it is this logic that people mobilize when they are recounting events or telling stories. In this respect, Bruner (1991), a famous narratologist, notes that narratives can be characterized by 10 features, which he lists as: (1) narrative diachronicity; (2) particularity; (3) intentional state entailment; (4) hermeneutic composability; (5) canonicity and breach; (6) referentiality; (7) genericness; (8) normativeness; (9) context sensitivity and negotiability; and (10) narrative accrual. Since these features summarize very well some important aspects of narratives and storytelling, I will spend this whole section explaining and illustrating what they each consist of.

In order to do that, let us first look at the following excerpt taken from Cooren (2007), which illustrates the telling of a narrative in an organizational setting. Sam Steinberg is the CEO of a large Canadian grocery company, with headquarters in Montreal, Quebec. In this passage, he is telling a little story to make a point during a meeting of his top management team in which he is also a participant. We will concentrate especially on the anecdote he is recounting at the end of this excerpt, an anecdote that concerns one of his stores, called St-Lawrence and Cremazie, located in Montreal, Quebec. However, we will see something early on that is also interesting, as Jack Levine, the vice-president of the company's Quebec division (who also happens to be Sam's closest associate), corrects the numbers that his boss is putting forward.

Since I already showed you how conversation analysts transcribe interactions, I will use their conventions to reproduce this conversation.

64	Sam:	This is exactly how I feel. (0.5) Now listen to what I'm telling, each and
65		every one of you. (0.5) Evidently over the past four or five weeks, (0.5) a
66		hundred items (0.5) had to be increased in price.
67	Jack:	<Seventy-two items>=
68	Sam:	=Alright, well, I'm telling you what I heard. [So-
69	Jack:	[accumulated on four weeks,
70		seventy-two items=
71	Sam:	=Okay. Let's (0.2) let's say it's seventy-two items. (1.0) So here's what
72		happens. I meet one of our managers having lunch upstairs, who's the

73	manager of St-Lawrence and Cremazie. I walked over an' say, "Hello,
74	how are you?" and everything else, "How is it going?" He says, "Very
75	fine, sales are up thirteen or fourteen percent," but he says he's terribly
76	disturbed. (0.5) They got in a wh:ole list of items that they have to
77	increase the prices on (0.5) and he's disturbed because now they'll be
78	going back to what they did in the past, erasing prices an' (.) putting on
79	higher prices an' everything else.

As illustrated in this excerpt, narrative diachronicity (1) means that a story is characterized by several events that are occurring over time (*dia* and *chronos* respectively mean "through" and "time" in Greek). Bruner notes that a narrative – here, Sam's anecdote – "is irreducibly durative" (p. 6), that is, it is marked by a beginning (Sam arriving on the premises of one of his stores), a middle (Sam meeting and then speaking with one of his managers), and an end (Sam learning about something disturbing that his manager is experiencing). Note that what precedes the anecdote per se (when Sam speaks about the price increase) is also marked by diachronicity, as we learn that the prices of several items have been increased over the past four to five weeks, information that provides the background of the story he is telling.

This excerpt also illustrates the second feature, *particularity* (2), to the extent that a narrative always is about *specific events that happened in specific circumstances*, even if this is to tell the story of a whole company facing harrowing times. In Sam Steinberg's case, it is about this particular event that took place, according to his account, in one of his stores, at St-Lawrence and Cremazie, a few days before the scheduled date of the top management meeting. Note in particular how Sam actually reproduces the conversation he had with his manager ("hello, how are you?" lines 73–4), so as to make it more real and present to his audience. Bruner also points out that, despite their particularity, narratives are characterized by their illustrative or emblematic dimension, which means that everybody is supposed to understand, especially the meeting participants who hear this account, that this story is meant to illustrate a more general and generic situation, which should concern them: the fact, which is mentioned by Sam

Steinberg at the beginning of his intervention, that his company is raising prices on several items (we will return to this point with respect to the seventh characteristic, i.e., *genericness*).

If you look carefully at this narrative, you will also see that the two protagonists of the story (Sam Steinberg and his manager) are presented as *affected* by what is happening. This means that a story is characterized by what Bruner (1991) lists as beliefs, desires, theories, values, and so on, which he calls *intentional states*. For instance, the manager is portrayed as "disturbed" and as telling Sam Steinberg *why* he is so: some of his expectations about prices were apparently not met in his store. By *intentional state entailment* (3), Bruner thus conveys the idea that a story is characterized by events that affect, concern, or disturb its protagonists, which then explains why they react in such and such ways. Another important narratologist, Algirdas Julien Greimas (1987), speaks of the agonistic or polemical dimension of narratives, which means that narratives are usually marked by forms of adversity and struggle, which can be resolved throughout the story (we will come back to this point later in the book).

If we now turn to the fourth feature – which Bruner calls *hermeneutic composability* (4) – we note that it invites us to identify the compositional nature of narrative interpretation (*hermeneu*, means "translating" or "interpreting" in Greek). In order to interpret Sam Steinberg's narrative, we indeed have to put together different parts of his account and relate them to each other so that they somehow hold together and make sense. But Bruner also notes the type of circle (also called hermeneutic circle) that is implied in this key activity, given that any part of Sam's narrative also makes sense because of its function or role in the whole story he is telling. Interpretation is therefore marked by a constant back-and-forth movement between the parts and the whole: the parts allow us to make sense of the whole, but the whole allows us to make sense of the parts.

Another key feature that Bruner mentions is *canonicity* and *breach* (5). What he means is that a story must be *tellable*: it must have a point, be relevant. Imagine a story in which Sam Steinberg recounts his conversation with his manager from the St-Lawrence and Cremazie store, but this time without any mention of a problem or issue (they just had a good time chatting to each other). We (and the members of his top management team) would then wonder why on earth he was telling this story! We might imagine that the fact they had a good time speaking with each other makes it tellable or worth telling, but would then wonder why "having a good time with this manager" constitutes some kind of event worth mentioning to his audience. We might also still wonder why he is telling this story at this point, that is, what makes it relevant to the subject currently being discussed by the top managers, which is the raising of prices on some items.

In order to have a story, there thus needs to be some kind of breach, violation, or infringement – something eventful to recount (Cooren, 2000; Greimas, 1987; Taylor and Van Every, 2000). In Sam Steinberg's story, the breach comes from the fact that one of his managers is disturbed by something that he does not like to do: raise prices in his store. The canonical script or program has been breached to the extent that a store is supposed to keep prices as low as possible (this is the canon, norm, or even law of this kind of store, especially Sam Steinberg's stores, which are renowned for their low prices throughout the year). This decision to raise prices, which comes from top management, is thus experienced as a form of infringement vis-à-vis this norm or canon, making this story worth telling: something is happening (a breach) that was not supposed to happen (according to the canons of the profession/organization).

Bruner also mentions the principle of referentiality (6) to point out that a story (even a fictional one) always *refers* to a specific situation, a situation that the narrative happens to *constitute* or *define*. Although the question of its truth or verisimilitude can always be present, especially when it is presented as a true story or anecdote, Bruner notes that stories have this capacity to *define* a specific situation by transforming a simple account into, for instance, the story of a betrayal or treason (some parallels with rhetoric can thus be drawn here). Raising prices, for example, could in some accounts be presented as uneventful, not worth mentioning, but the fact that Sam Steinberg makes it worth telling implies that he is referring to something problematic, which is relevant and therefore deserves to be addressed and solved by his organization.

In this regard, Bruner speaks of *genericness* (7) to highlight the generic or typical character of stories, something we already alluded to. By this, he means that a story tends to be categorized with respect to recognizable genres or models (for instance, comedies, tragedies, jokes, dramas, anecdotes, etc.), but that these categories also help us make sense of its relevance. In Sam Steinberg's case, we understand that this anecdote is meant to illustrate something that might be *typical* of his organization in its present state. It is therefore what makes his story relevant and therefore tellable. It is certainly a little story, an anecdote, but it indicates that something is going wrong in his organization, something that might be consequential in terms of profitability or even survival for his company.

But if narratives have a generic dimension and need to be tellable, it is also because of another characteristic, which Bruner calls *normativeness* (8). We have already remarked on the moral character of a story, which means that narratives always come with some kind of uptake, significance, or relevance. Something happened that was not supposed to happen, that is, some norms, canons, principles, or rules were broken or violated. Importantly, a narrative even has this capacity to renew or modify the way people think about situations. For instance, even if price increases were considered something perfectly normal or uneventful to his interlocutors, the very fact that Sam mentioned this anecdote implies that *this is not the case for him* (and therefore that this should not be the case for them!). We thus see, again, how narratives *constitute* situations, especially in terms of normative expectations. In the context of this top management meeting, this situation is constituted or defined as problematic, at least by Sam Steinberg.

This question of normativeness allows us to introduce the next to last characteristic, which Bruner calls *context sensitivity and negotiability* (9). By this, he means that narratives are and should always be considered *perspectives* on specific situations (whether fictional or real) and that these perspectives can be negotiated in interaction. Because of their normative or evaluative character, narratives thus function as standpoints, viewpoints, or positions vis-à-vis a specific issue. To a narrative, someone can thus respond with a *counternarrative*, which might then come with another moral and even another breach.

Look, for instance, at the way Jack Levine, the vice-president of the Quebec division, responds just after hearing what Sam had to say.

87	Jack L:	Mr president look, this is what – This's why I want to talk about structure
88		first. (1.0) it happens that I and you communicate. (0.5) >twice a day three
89		time a day four times a day – no matter what time of day it is, eh?<
90	Sam S:	Ri[ght
91	Jack L:	[We communicate, I communicate to you, you com'nicate to
92		me. And I brought up to you (1.0) this perplex thing. 'Cause I have to
93		have somebody to speak to too (.) outside of my peers who we speak to,
94		eh? So I communicate with this ((spoken with intensity and pointing
95		finger)). Have you got the same problem in Toronto?
96		(1.0)
97	Jack L:	Do you know what's happening at Toron[to?
98	Sam S:	[No, I don't
99	Jack L:	((spoken with intensity and pointing finger)) Are you running one
100		company or two companies?

As we see, Jack Levine counterattacks with another account, which implies, of course, another moral, another normativeness (Taylor and Robichaud, 2007). This reaction is not surprising to the extent that he is, as mentioned before, the person in charge of directly supervising the manager of the St-Lawrence and Cremazie store (as the vice-president of the Quebec division, he is accountable for the whole Montreal sector). He therefore cannot help but hear Sam's anecdote as an implicit *critique* addressed to his area of responsibility.

So how does he respond? As he points out, he and Sam Steinberg communicate quite often with each other (three or four times a day), something that Sam himself confirms. This explains why Jack knows about this price situation, which he presents as something he even brought up to his boss. This situation is therefore *tellable* (as he tells it, it is a perplexing thing), but for Jack, it has a different moral or uptake. It tells something different about his organization, which is that top managers, especially Sam, do not really know what is happening in other parts of their organization ("Do you know what's happening at Toronto?" (line 97), "Are you running one company or two companies?" (lines 100–1)).

In other words, this anecdote told by Sam illustrates for Jack Levine the kind of one-to-one style of leadership that Sam exerts in his company. Sam knows what is happening in this specific store because he happened to have a conversation with this manager, but he does not "know what's happening at Toronto," which leads Jack to ask his (rhetorical) question: "Are you running one company or two companies?" Jack therefore reinterprets this anecdote as illustrating the lack of structure that this company is suffering from, a lack of structure that explains that some problems get communicated (through one-to-one conversations), while others remain unknown. What Sam's story says, what it means, what its moral is, can always be the object of negotiations or even, as we see here, polemics or debates.

As for the last feature, which Bruner calls *narrative accrual* (10), it invites us to pay attention to the cumulative character of stories and anecdotes. As we will later see, some (types of) narratives tend to be *cultivated* in organizations or societies, which means that they tend to be repeated over and over, an activity that amounts to reproducing the norms, values, standards, rules, or canons that these narratives implicitly or explicitly defend. An organizational culture is thus characterized by the type of stories that people tell, since the telling of these stories says something about the kind of values, norms, or standards that are promoted in a given organization. Narratives thus *reaffirm* what, in many respects, define and constitute an organization, that is, its rules, canons, and norms (Mumby, 1988).

Critical Discourse Analysis

Let us now turn to the final perspective, that is, critical discourse analysis, hereafter CDA. If we briefly compare it with the five others, we can first observe that this one is characterized by its critical, denunciative, or normative agenda. What does it mean? Simply that critical discourse analysts are not merely interested in analyzing how discourse works or what it does, but also aim at *denouncing* or *critiquing* forms of power, control, dominance, inequality, or oppression that language use contributes to reproducing. Given this normative agenda of denunciation, critical discourse analysts thus implicitly or explicitly defend what Teun van Dijk (1993) would call an "applied ethics" (p. 253), that is, various conceptions about what would be the conditions for a better and fairer society (and therefore the conditions for better and fairer organizations). As van Dijk points out, "CDA is unabashedly normative" (p. 253).

Of course, representatives of other perspectives, such as rhetoric and semiotics, can sometimes develop a critical agenda – for instance, Charland's (1987) constitutive rhetoric or Robert Hodge and Günther Kress's (1988) social semiotics – but CDA, as a specific approach to discourse, is first and foremost marked by this objective of denunciation, as well as by a general attitude of suspicion (Mumby, 1997). This means that many different approaches to discourse analysis can be developed under this umbrella term. Teun van Dijk (1993) writes, for example, that "CDA should deal primarily with the discourse dimensions of power abuse and the injustice and inequality that result from it" (p. 252), which implies that any approach to discourse analysis that would aim at revealing these dimensions of power abuse could claim to be (or be considered) critical.

In this section, I will thus introduce you to key figures of CDA, that is, scholars whose work has, over the years, been implicitly or explicitly associated with this movement of research. These scholars do not necessarily agree with each other, but their respective contributions are all characterized by this normative agenda, a general attitude of suspicion and denunciation, and a fundamental concern for social change (Fairclough, 1992).

Historically, two French philosophers have been retrospectively associated with CDA as a research movement: one who represents the Marxist tradition, Louis Althusser (1918–90), and another who somehow managed to invent his own tradition, Michel Foucault (1926–84), who is also identified as an historian of ideas. Michel Foucault was Althusser's disciple at the École Normale Supérieure, a prestigious academic institution in Paris, but quickly became disenchanted with Marxism, which led him to develop his own research agenda and methodology.

Beyond their differences, both were interested in activities or processes of *subjection*, that is, the conditions by which someone becomes a subject. Although the term "subject" is sometimes used as synonymous for "actor" or "agent," Foucault and Althusser highlight the etymological root of this notion by noting that a subject is first and foremost a person who is *subjected* to someone or something else (the Latin root *subiectus* indeed means to throw (jet) under (sub)). In other words, a subject is someone who is acted upon or submitted to someone or something else.

In order to convey this idea of subjection, Althusser (1971) proposes the term "interpellation," which can mean, depending on the context, "calling out to someone," "questioning someone," or "hailing someone."[5] In a famous scene that Althusser imagines, he stages a policeman who is hailing someone by saying "Hey, you there!" As he writes,

> Assuming that the theoretical scene I have imagined takes place in the street, the hailed individual will turn round. By this mere one-hundred-and-eighty-degree physical conversion, he becomes a *subject*. Why? Because he has recognized that the hail was 'really' addressed to him, and that "it was *really him* who was hailed" (and not someone else). (p. 174; italics in the original)

Through this illustration, Althusser intends to show that *ideology* hails or interpellates individuals *as subjects*.

What is an ideology for Althusser? It is, as he points out, "a representation of the imaginary relationship of individuals to their real conditions of existence" (p. 162). In other words, ideologies can be considered as sets of ideas (beliefs, assumptions, norms, values, etc.) to which individuals are subjected and that hide the real character of their conditions. The policeman implicitly embodies a form of ideology, which "has the function (which defines it) of 'constituting' concrete individuals as subjects" (p. 171). Through the policeman and his interpellation, the person is therefore subjected to a specific ideology – what Althusser calls "the state ideology" – that the policeman represents.

What does this mean in practice? First, it is noteworthy that hailing someone in the street – especially when it comes from a policeman – is not something neutral or unbiased. It implicitly positions or defines the subject of this interpellation as having maybe done something wrong (he or she is at least suspected of something). This means that subjection is associated here with something negative, either because the person is being falsely accused of something she has not done or because she has actually committed something that is considered wrong (but the question then becomes: *who* or *what* is allowed to define what is right and what is wrong).

Second, this scene also shows that becoming the subject of interpellation is something very concrete that is irremediably linked with an act of communication or discourse: "Hey, you there!" Given what you have already read in one of the previous sections, we could even speak of a *speech act*, which transforms the individual subjected to it: the person is now considered interpellated, which means that, to any witness, she is already being considered potentially guilty of something.

Althusser (1971) then points out that, in fact, we are *always already* interpellated by ideologies, not only from birth, but even before. For instance, as an unborn baby, we were already the subjects of (i.e., subjected to) specific discourses and conversations (from our parents, siblings, relatives, etc.), which for Althusser demonstrates that ideological subjection starts before we are actually born. A critical perspective on discourse is thus meant to reveal and denounce these activities of subjection, which Althusser considers to be *invisible* to most subjects. As he notes, an ideology recruits subjects by interpellating them, but "one of the effects of ideology is the practical *denegation* of the ideological character of ideology by ideology: ideology never says 'I am ideological'" (p. 175).

Similar ideas can be found in the work of his disciple, Michel

Foucault, but with important differences that I will now outline briefly. First, a major difference is that Foucault (1984) rejects the term "ideology," which implies for him an absolute distinction between what would be considered scientific, rational, or true vs. what would be believed to be ideological, irrational, or false (an opposition that is indeed explicitly made by Althusser in his writings). Foucault thus shows that we are indeed subjected to ways of thinking or systems of thought (remember that he is an historian of ideas), but that *there is no way to escape this condition*. Our subjection is therefore *constitutive* of what we are, and the best we can do is to analyze where different types of subjection lead us to as individuals, organizations, and societies.

Instead of speaking of "ideology," Foucault first proposed the term "episteme" (Foucault, 1970/1989), and then later the notions of "discursive formation" (Foucault, 1977b) and "regimes of truth" (Foucault, 1977a). Although they differ from each other in some important aspects, these terminologies all roughly refer to a set of presuppositions, assumptions, norms, rules, or beliefs that are supposed to distinguish what is considered to be true or right from what is considered to be false or wrong (*episteme* means knowledge in Greek).

As subjects, we are therefore submitted to various regimes of truth, various discursive formations that have been developed and institutionalized over the years and that people implicitly or explicitly reproduce in their conversations, conducts, and practices. Foucault was especially interested in the regimes of truth that were developed throughout the centuries (especially from the seventeenth century) and that were constitutive of disciplines like medicine, education, or law. For instance, he compared the way individuals were executed until the middle of the eighteenth century with the way they were disciplined less than a hundred years later (Foucault, 1977a).

Another important aspect that distinguishes Foucault from Althusser is that Foucault does not necessarily consider that subjection is something wrong or that needs to be systematically battled against (although he would certainly call for a form of systematic vigilance). As already pointed out, he notes that we cannot escape our condition of being subjects, which means that regimes of truth should be analyzed in terms of the type of subject they produce or constitute. While Althusser and Marxists in general tend to denounce what they consider to be the repressive or oppressive characters of ideologies, Foucault notes that any regime of truth, any discursive formation produces certain types of subjects and that these subjects are not only constrained, but also *empowered* by them.

For instance, Karen Ashcraft (2000, 2005) very nicely shows how feminist principles not only constrain, but also empower organizational members regarding how they deal with daily affairs, especially key questions such as the way in which private matters merge with public life, or power abuse. We can therefore speak of a certain form of relativism on Foucault's part to the extent that a priori, no specific regime of truth can be considered superior to another (see especially Foucault, 1977a).

As we see through the figures of its two founding fathers, Althusser and Foucault, CDA is characterized by its focus on what Gee (1999), as well as Alvesson and Kärreman (2000), identified as big D discourse (see chapter 1). For instance, Althusser is interested in what he calls the "Christian religious ideology" or the "Capitalist ideology," while Foucault analyzes the succession (or cohabitation) of several epistemes, discursive formations, or regimes of truth throughout the centuries. Although the terminology to speak about what is happening varies, the focus of the analysis remains the same, less on the events of communication per se (small d discourse) than ultimately concentrated on the ideologies or regimes of truth that are reproduced, altered, or confirmed through these events of communication.

Foucault, for instance, would say that when a doctor is speaking to a patient in the context of a medical consultation, it is not only a doctor who is actually talking, but also a specific regime of truth that is expressing and reproducing itself, a regime of truth to which *both* the patient *and* the doctor are subjected. For instance, some specific topics will be deemed acceptable by the physician, while others will not. The question of patient empowerment – the patients' right to participate in decisions made about their own health – is a good example where doctors and patients might differ about what is considered acceptable.

Given its focus on subjection, what also characterizes CDA is its interest in *power* relations. As Wodak (1999) notes, "interaction always involves power and ideologies. No interaction exists in which power relations do not prevail and in which values and norms do not have a relevant role" (p. 186). In addition to focusing on what is happening in a given discourse or interaction, critical scholars thus analyze what they call their *conditions of possibility* (Fairclough, 2005), that is, what makes a certain interaction or discourse possible not only in terms of what is said and how it is said, but also in terms of *who* is authorized or constrained to say it and what authorizes or constrains this person to say what she says.

For instance, in a supervisor/supervisee interaction, a critical scholar would focus not only on what the supervisor and the supervisee are telling each other, but also on how this interaction reproduces specific relations of power and domination between them. When studying what is said and how it is said, they would notice, for instance, that the supervisor *typically* tells her supervisee what to do, while the supervisee simply acknowledges what is requested from him and then acts accordingly, that is, does what he was asked to do. This is, of course, just an example, as more complex forms of interaction could be envisaged. For example, a critical analyst could also be interested in forms of *resistance* that are subtly deployed by the supervisee in order to mark what he considers to be the limit of his boss's authority (Mumby, 2005).

Norman Fairclough (1992, 1995, 2005), who is certainly the most renowned scholar associated with CDA, proposes a three-dimensional conception of discourse, which he calls text-oriented discourse analysis (TODA). For him, discourse should be analyzed not only as (1) *a text*, which he identifies as anything that is said or written, but also as (2) *a discursive practice*, which he globally characterizes as text production and interpretation, and (3) *a social practice*, which he also defines as the political, organizational, cultural, or ideological dimension of discourse, that is, the extent to which discourse contributes to reproducing or altering specific ideological, organizational, cultural, and political structures.

For instance, if we return to the top management meeting we briefly analyzed in the previous section on narrative analysis, we notice that the *textual* dimension of discourse corresponds to what Sam Steinberg, Jack Levine, and other top managers are saying in the context of this meeting (and how they are saying what they are saying). This would then correspond to the transcript that reproduces this discussion without any information about intonations, gazes, gestures, etc. As for discourse taken as a *discursive practice*, it refers not only to how participants produce and interpret the texts that constitute their exchange, but also to what specific discourses (or I should say Discourses, with a big D) are being reproduced, borrowed, or altered during this discussion, what Fairclough also calls "orders of discourse," an expression he borrows directly from Foucault (1981).

In the case of the top management meeting, we can notice, for instance, that what both Sam Steinberg and Jack Levine say tends to reproduce a typical *genre* or order of discourse, which is characterized by specific preoccupations or concerns: sales that are increasing, managers that are complaining, prices on items that are too high, and what Jack presents as structural problems within the company. From all the things that are happening in their organization, this is what appears to concern or preoccupy them at this point, which leads them to reiterate what could be called a *typical managerial discourse*, a discourse where only specific concerns are made present, while others are silenced (for instance, at no moment do we hear in the entire meeting any references to employees and their concerns, see Deetz et al., 2007).

But beyond this homogeneous view of what is happening, Fairclough would point out that discursive practices are also marked by heterogeneity and relations of power. Although it is difficult to illustrate this aspect with only the two excerpts commented on in the previous section, a more thorough and longitudinal analysis of this top management meeting would show that Sam Steinberg's discourse tends to implicitly voice and reproduce a traditional conception of management (for more details, see

Cooren, 2007). It is a form of management consisting of informal conversations with managers, personal relationships with employees, intuitive decisions, and nepotism (Sam Steinberg is a self-made man who built a grocery empire from a family business, which certainly explains this dimension of his discourse).

In opposition to this traditional discourse, another – here embodied in Jack Levine's turn of talk – insists, on the contrary, on the importance of providing a clear structure to the organization, hiring top managers with business school credentials, and getting clear channels of command and control. This discourse tends to implicitly voice and reproduce what we could call a professional and modern conception of management, which many top managers round the table are defending at the time of this discussion. As we see through this example, a CDA approach thus insists that it is not only a matter of people who are talking to each other in this kind of meeting, but also Discourses (Foucault would say regimes of truth or discursive formations) that are opposing each other.

Finally, Fairclough (2005) notes that these discursive practices participate in the reproduction and/or transformation of *social practices*, the third dimension of his model. This distinction is important for him, as he points out that any discursive practice is a social practice, but that any social practice is not necessarily a discursive practice. Here, Fairclough notes that the production of commodities, often the central activity of any organization, is a social practice that cannot be reduced to a discursive practice, even if it includes discursive components (to coordinate activities, for instance). Think of the production of cellphones in a telephone company and you will have an idea of what he means: the activity of assembling telephones is a social/organizational practice that cannot be reduced to the interactions that take place to coordinate these activities.

According to Fairclough (1993), any discursive practice is therefore *constitutive* of organizational forms (it defines situations, initiates programs of action, commits people to doing things, etc.), but he implicitly notes the *hybrid* character of organizations (Cooren, 2006), which cannot be *reduced* to what people say and write. Organizations are indeed made of discourses, titles, organizational charts, statuses, decisions, and human interactions (which are literally made of or fabricated with language), but they are also made of buildings, machines, capital, commodities, techniques, technological networks, and land properties, which mobilize language in order to exist, but cannot be reduced, *as a product*, to language per se. As he notes, language use or discourse "is socially shaped, but it is also socially shaping, or *constitutive*" (p. 134).

A Synthesis?

Now that we have been introduced to these six perspectives, we could wonder if there is not any way to articulate them with each other. This would allow us to offer a sort of synthesis that would demonstrate how these perspectives are, in fact, talking about the same thing, but seen from different angles, which leads them to highlight various aspects of the phenomenon they are analyzing. Recall the analogy of the blind men that I used at the end of the previous chapter: these six perspectives are all claiming to be analyzing discourse (our elephant), but they do not appear to be focusing on the same aspect or part of this reality, which leads them to say different things about what it is and how it works.

For example, we saw that *semiotics* insists that the world around us is not only meaningful, but is also actively *telling us* things that we can interpret. Interpreting our environment thus means that we reconstruct what it tells or communicates to us, whether it is through a sign posted on a wall, a diagram that we have to decode, or a person who is talking to us. We also saw that semiotics allows us to acknowledge the *hybrid* character of organizational forms, which, as we just saw, parallels what CDA is putting forward. An organization is not just made of people talking, writing, or, more generally, communicating to each other; it is also made of buildings, land properties, technologies, capital, etc. What semiotics reminds us, however, is that all these things can literally speak to us – that is, tell us things that are constitutive of the ways organizations are, work, act, and function (or dysfunction).

Many things (whatever they are: a logo, a turn of talk, an

architectural element) thus play a role in the structuring and organizing of collective forms (Latour, 1996). In other words, they display a form of *agency*, that is, they literally *do things*, and it is this agency that constitutes organizational forms (Cooren, 2006). Although our second perspective, *rhetoric*, rarely focuses on things and their persuasive or influential power (but see Burke, 1945/1962), rhetoricians' take on discourse and communication is not incompatible with semiotics. What rhetoric reminds us especially is that whoever or whatever is telling us something, this telling amounts to explicitly or implicitly *defining a situation* in a specific way, hence its constitutive power.

Interestingly, this rhetorical view is not incompatible with what CDA is saying about subjection. Whenever a discourse is produced, it tends to subject individuals to a specific situation, be it when people are just talking about the weather, when a communiqué is released in response to a disaster, or when someone asks another person to complete a task. Discourse, as pointed out by rhetoric, is also a way to imply or pinpoint what counts or matters in a given context, which parallels what narratologists have been saying about the selective or defining character of sense-making activities, especially when people tell stories or anecdotes. This also confirms what conversation analysts and ethnomethodologists are saying about the *reflexive* character of discourse and interaction. Discourse is reflexive to the extent that *what people do, say*, or *write* in a situation actively participates in the definition, production, and even constitution of that very situation.

To this, we could add what speech act theory insists on, which is that discourse not only defines, produces, or constitutes; it also *transforms* the world in which we evolve: people are getting married, facts are being reasserted, commitments are made, and so on. This means that even when we feel that something is getting reproduced, reiterated, or confirmed (e.g., the institution of marriage, a given scientific theory, or a political engagement), it means that this reproduction or confirmation is, in itself, an act or an event. Garfinkel (2002), the founding father of ethnomethodology, has a very nice expression to summarize this paradox. He says that anything that people do happens "for another next first time," which marks the iterable and eventful character of (social and organizational) life in general, including routines and procedures. In other words, even reproduction and reiteration imply that something is done, which presupposes a transformation, that is, an action, as minimal as it may seem.

Speaking of conversation analysts and ethnomethodologists, we saw that their contribution to discourse analysis especially consists of highlighting the *accountable* dimension of people's conducts. People and their actions or discourse are indeed constituting, defining, and transforming situations, but their actions and discourse are also accountable. This means that people can question, negotiate, assess, or confirm what is taking place in a specific situation. A social or organizational world is therefore co-constructed or co-constituted through discourse and interaction, and participants are constantly orienting to its normative or accountable character.

As pointed out, stories, anecdotes, and narratives in general not only define situations, but also reaffirm, implicitly or explicitly, specific norms, standards, or values. What narrative analysis also reminds us is that the discourse people produce (whether it is a story, an argument, or a simple point being made) can always be reinterpreted by others, which shows that people never fully control how their discourse will be understood and what it might be made to say. Sam Steinberg wanted to make a point with his little anecdote, but we saw how Jack Levine was quickly able to show what, for him, this little anecdote was actually saying about their organization.

This brings us to the sixth perspective, critical discourse analysis, which rightly points out that when people talk, write, or communicate in general, it is not only they who are expressing themselves, but also specific ideologies or regimes of truth that define situations in a specific way. It is not only Sam Steinberg who is speaking when he is telling his story, but also a way of conceiving the (organizational) world, which is immediately countered by another conception, embodied and translated through Jack Levine's reaction. How can it be so? Because any human actor is, by definition, inhabited or animated by specific preoccupations, concerns, or even obsessions about what is supposed to *count* or *matter* in a given situation (Cooren, 2010), which echoes what rhetoric has to say about discourse.

We do not choose what preoccupies or concerns us; it just does and this is why nobody can be in total control of what he or she says, writes, or communicates in general, which echoes what the five other perspectives also say and show, each in their own way. Our discourse thus conveys, for another next first time, our values, convictions, ideologies, and obsessions, and this is what CDA also allows us to see and analyze.

So does it mean that, "Everything is fine, everything goes fine, everything is in the best possible way," as Voltaire's Candide naively declares? No, as each of these perspectives, of course, disagree on many points. How could they not, given that what counts or matters differs for each of them (for an interesting comparison between some of these perspectives, see Craig, 1999). But I believe that beyond these disagreements, some passage points can be found and that each of them has something interesting to tell us about discourse. This is what I propose to summarize in table 2.1.

Structure of the Remaining Chapters

With table 2.1 in mind, we now start to see what we can actually do with these six analytical perspectives. This is what I propose to show you in the remaining chapters of this book. As you will notice, these chapters not only address various topics – "Coordination and Organizing" (chapter 3), "Organizational Culture, Identity, and Ideology" (chapter 4), and "Meetings: Negotiation, Decision-making, and Conflicts" (chapter 5) – but also follow a line of progression in the way discourse analysis is presented. This should hopefully facilitate your learning process as you progressively come to master this way of analyzing organizational life.

In chapter 3 ("Coordination and Organizing"), the interaction analyzed will be relatively simple to help you start to gradually understand the constitutive role discourse plays in the

Table 2.1 The six perspectives: conceptions, research agendas, central ideas, and constitutive views of discourse.

Perspectives	Discourse as	Agenda	Central idea	Constitutive view of discourse
Semiotics	signs	Analyzing the functioning of signs, i.e., how they tell us what they tell us	Discourse should not be limited to what people say. *Other things tell us things.*	Discourses (icons, indexes or symbols) organize and structure our world
Rhetoric	persuasion, inducement, or influence	Analyzing how people manage to influence, persuade, or even constitute their audience	Discourse implicitly or explicitly defines what *counts or matters* in a given situation	By defining situations, discourse constitutes specific identities, which commit people to doing certain things
Speech act theory	an act	Analyzing how people do things with words (asserting, committing oneself, directing, expressing, declaring, etc.)	Discourse consists of a series of *acts that transform the world*, as minimal and iterative as these transformations might be	Discourse transforms situations by mobilizing and invoking various sources of authority
Ethnomethodology and conversation analysis	a conduct	Analyzing what people do and are up to in interaction and how they do what they do	Discourse reflexively and accountably contributes to the *co-enactment of the social world*	Any situation is at least partly defined and constituted by the way people enact, orient to, and make sense of it
Narrative analysis	narrative sequences	Analyzing the structure and functioning of narratives	Discourse *has a life/logic of its own* and always has a *normative* component	Narratives constitute what defines an organization, i.e., its rules, canons, and norms
Critical discourse analysis (CDA)	Ideologies and regimes of truth	Denouncing the ideological dimensions of discourse in order to strive for social change	Discourse is an activity of *subjection*, both for the author and the hearers/readers	Any discourse is *constitutive* of organizations but the latter cannot be reduced to discourse

enactment of organizational processes. The situation – a group of friends helping one of them move from her apartment – will also have the characteristic of being somehow *pre-organizational* in that this group does not constitute a formal organization per se. Throughout this chapter, I will alternatively mobilize each perspective to highlight various aspects of the interaction and show what each can tell us about coordinating and organizing in general. In order to facilitate the reading, I will indicate the specific perspective that we are using by putting its name in bold when I start mobilizing it (this convention will also be used throughout the remaining chapters).

In chapter 4 ("Organizational Culture, Identity, and Ideology"), we will increase the difficulty somewhat by reproducing a specific interaction that took place in a formal organization. From a group of friends getting organized to complete a specific task, we will switch to self-management team members addressing the alleged wrongdoings of which one of them is accused. Although this situation definitely takes place *in* a formal organization that is already established, this chapter will allow us to decipher to what extent this type of discourse participates in the constitution of a specific organizational culture, identity, and ideology.

Finally, chapter 5 ("Meetings: Negotiation, Decision-making, and Conflicts") will allow you to test your indepth comprehension of each perspective. In this section, six successive excerpts of a single meeting will be reproduced, each being analyzed from one of the six perspectives (rhetoric, semiotics, speech act theory, conversation analysis/ethnomethodology, narrative analysis, and critical discourse analysis). In contrast to the two previous chapters, this one will offer you the opportunity to see in fuller detail the complexity and richness of discourse in interaction. It is my belief that by the end of this chapter, you should be well equipped to deal with discourse from a constitutive perspective.

3

Coordination and Organizing

In this chapter, I will show you what discourse analysis has to tell us about an important trait shared by all organizational forms – the fact that they are organized or structured! From this, the question arises as to what it means to have something organized or to organize something. In this respect, Gilles Deleuze and Félix Guattari (1987) note that organizing consists of providing or creating organs for a given body, a body (and this is the paradox) that will be defined, identified, and delimitated, at least partly, by the organs that are produced in its name (Bencherki and Cooren, 2011). By "body," they not only mean a biological form (the body of an animal or plant), but also a social form, as when we speak of a governmental or institutional body, for instance.

This sounds like a very complex idea, but just imagine a bunch of pals (let's call them Joey, Patrick, and Amy) who are getting together in order to help a common friend (let's call her Julia) move from her apartment. Chances are that they will begin the whole process by *getting organized* in order to be as effective as possible with their project. Concretely, it might mean that one person will be asked to divide labor between the four individuals. Let's say this is Julia, given that she is the one who is moving, a situation that gives her a form of natural authority (but it could be someone else, for instance, a person who is considered to have some experience with moving).

In response to this request, Julia might, for example, propose that Joey and Patrick be in charge of moving the boxes to the truck, and that Amy remain in the truck in order to place (and organize!) the boxes in the vehicle. Meanwhile, Julia would tell Joey and Patrick what boxes they can take to the truck while she finishes packing everything in her apartment. Clearly, getting organized in this specific case means that a *division of labor* is taking place, which implies that individuals are given specific functions, tasks, or roles, and that some coordination of the activities takes place (Mintzberg, 1973; Quinn and Dutton, 2005), what John Shotter (1984, 1993) also calls *joint actions*.

Initially, we simply had a group of people who had agreed to get together to fulfill a specific objective: helping one of them move from her apartment (we could call this group, echoing Deleuze and Guattari (1987), a "body without organs"). However, what we progressively see happening is that this group, this body, this whole, starts to differentiate itself: two persons (Joey and Patrick) are now in charge of moving the boxes to the truck; a third person (Amy) is responsible for placing the boxes in the truck; and a fourth person (Julia herself) is in charge of finishing packing while telling the first two what can be taken to the vehicle. The group thus is given organs to the extent that it is now differentiated into parts whose functions are to accomplish specific actions for the group itself.

Parts, whole, functions ... at first sight, we seem far away from discourse and interaction analysis. Indeed, this type of vocabulary echoes systems theory (Contractor and Seibold, 1993; Katz and Kahn, 1966; Luhmann, 1995; Rice and Cooper, 2010), a tradition of research that until recently was not so interested in language and discourse (but see Maturana, 1991; Schoeneborn, 2011; Taylor, 1995). However, what is important here is that we should be able to show how this differentiation is discursively accomplished, constituted, or performed on the terra firma of interaction. What also needs to be shown is that such differentiation *could fail at any moment* and that there is no harmonizing force that could explain the ins and outs of this differentiation (Tarde, 1895/2012).

Indeed, the problem with systems theory is that at least some versions of it tend to take the system itself for granted, which amounts to saying that somewhere there is a sort of force that would hold its parts together. As we will show, such a harmonizing force does not exist, since any system is at the mercy of all the actions that painstakingly and repeatedly maintain its form (Cooren and Robichaud, 2010). As John Shotter (1993) reminds us about joint actions:

> As people coordinate their activity with the activities of others, and 'respond' to them in what they do, what they as individuals desire and what actually results in their exchanges are often two very different things. In short, joint action produces *unintended* and unpredictable outcomes. (p. 39; italics in the original)

This does not mean there is no such thing as a system; it just means that any system needs to be *performed into being*, so to speak, which means that coordination is something that can fail and has to be constantly reproduced and reaffirmed in interaction. We will now see what this means.

The Organizing Property of Discourse

It is important to remember what **semiotics** taught us – that if there is such a thing as organizing, it is because specific actors, whether humans, technological, or even textual, *produced* or *performed* it. In our illustration, some kind of organizing is taking place because Julia was implicitly asked to divide labor between her friends. In order to do that, it is necessary to communicate, in this case, *tell others what they have to do*. This is something that Ludwig Wittgenstein (1953), the famous analytical philosopher, understood very well. And in order to be as specific as possible, let us imagine that Julia's friends all arrived one by one in her apartment. After having a chance to greet each other, the following interaction takes place:

1	Joey:	OK, Julia, how do you think we should proceed?
2	Julia:	Well, I don't know. Why don't you and Patrick take care of bringing
3		the boxes to the truck?
4	Patrick:	Sounds good ((nodding while looking at Joey, who also nods in sign
5		of agreement))

6	Julia	Great! ((turning to Amy)) Meanwhile, Amy, would you mind
7		placing the boxes that Joey and Patrick will bring you to the back of
8		the vehicle?
9	Amy	That's fine with me ((nodding))
10	Julia	OK.
11		(1.0)
12	Patrick:	OK. Which boxes should we start with?
13	Julia:	You could start with the boxes that are in the bedroom, if it's okay
14		with you. On my side, I will finish making the boxes in the
15		apartment.
16	Amy:	OK, so I am gonna be in the truck waiting for you, guys.
17	Joey:	OK, let's do it

In terms of constitution, we see that differentiation is indeed taking place because Julia decided to distribute various tasks among her friends. There was no instance of group structure, system, organs, or organization before Joey asked her, in the name of the group, how she wanted to proceed (line 1). We thus see in this example that if there is such a thing as a structure or organization, it needs to be *communicatively achieved and constituted*, which means that people have to talk to each other in order to organize themselves and constitute an organizational form (Cooren and Fairhurst, 2004). The question is, of course, how this is happening, and this is where discourse analysis becomes interesting.

Following Buckley (1967), the label "double interacts" is used by Karl E. Weick (1979) in his seminal book on the social psychology of organizing, for these sequences of joint actions where an actor A triggers a specific response in actor B (interact), which is then responded to by actor A (double interact). A double interact constitutes, for him, the essence of organizing. Why is it so? If we look at the interaction that is taking place between the four friends, we see that organizing indeed starts when Joey asks Julia how she thinks they should proceed for the moving (line 1), a request that prompts her to propose that he and Patrick take care of bringing the boxes to the truck (lines 2–3). Her proposition is then accepted by Patrick when this latter responds "Sounds good" on line 4, an agreement that is also confirmed and marked by the fact that both he and Joey nod upon hearing what Julia has to propose.

Each of these three **speech acts** ((1) Joey's question; (2) Julia's proposition; (3) Patrick's acceptance) contributes to the development of a first double interact where some form of *closure* (Cooren and Fairhurst, 2004) appears to be completed, a closure that precisely marks the achievement of this double interact. Why can we speak in terms of closure or conclusion? Precisely because the problem or question that was raised by Joey's intervention on line 1 ("OK, Julia, how do you think we should proceed?") can now be considered at least partly *solved* or *resolved* when both Patrick and Joey mark their agreement on line 4. They agree and now know that their role and task will be to bring the boxes to the truck during the upcoming hours, as proposed by Julia. Note, however, that the closure is relative to the extent that Amy still does not know what she should do (we will come back to this point later).

At this point, we observe that organizing takes place when some kind of problem has to be solved or some objective has to be achieved, whether collectively or individually. **Ethnomethodologically** speaking, we thus realize that organizing is something that has to be accomplished *by the interactants themselves.* Even the existence of a "group of friends" is something that is marked and *brought into being* in the interaction itself (Latour, 2005). For instance, Joey says, "How do you think *we* should proceed?", a question that, as noted before, implicitly positions Joey himself as speaking in the name of a "we," which is the group (or at least the sub-group made of the three friends that Julia called for help). As noted by Taylor and Van Every (2011), a group – or any kind of collective for that matter, even a couple – has to be *talked into being* in order to be recognized as such (Heritage, 1984).

By "talked into being," an expression that at first sight appears complex, we mean that this "group of friends," this "we," is something that was implicitly or explicitly created and constituted when Julia initially asked Joey, Patrick, and Amy to help her move from her apartment. From an ethnomethodological viewpoint, if we can, as observers and analysts, talk about something like a *group*, it is because this group was *reflexively* and *incarnatedly*[1] enacted, mobilized, and made visible in people's conversation, that is, talked into being, whether implicitly or explicitly. In other words, if such a thing called a group does exist, it is because participants mark and reaffirm its existence through what they say or do (Latour, 2005). By asking her friends Joey, Patrick, and Amy to help her move from her apartment, Julia implicitly constitutes a "them," which is asked to do something for her, an action that amounts to defining a group, a "we," endowed with a specific task (Taylor and Van Every, 2011).

But note, and this is the interesting part, that the same logic obtains for the so-called "parts" or subgroups of the group. We just saw that the existence of the group itself was implicitly reaffirmed when Joey, using the pronoun "we," talked on its behalf in his question to Julia on line 1. But we can now see how Julia, in responding to Joey, implicitly proposes the creation of a first organ, a first part, a first subgroup, which will be in charge of a specific task ("Well, I don't know. Why don't *you* and Patrick take care of bringing the boxes to the truck?" lines 2–3). With this response, a "you" is now identified and proposed within the "we."

Thanks to **speech act theory**, we already know that language not only allows us to refer to or talk about things in the world (*constatives*), but also participates in the transformation of this very world (*performatives*). As Austin (1962) brilliantly showed us, people *do things* with words. On lines 2 and 3, Julia not only tells Patrick and Joey what they could do, but also constitutes or defines them as a "you," a subgroup in the group (or a sub-we in the we, if you will), what we already called an organ. Why can it be considered an organ? Because this new "you," which did not exist before it was identified by Julia, is proposed to be in charge of a specific function or task for the group itself.

Interestingly, we also see that it is Patrick, and not Joey, who responds, "Sounds good" on line 4, marking his agreement with what Julia just proposed. As he nods while saying this, he looks at Joey as if to check that the latter also agrees with what Julia proposes, an agreement that is confirmed when Joey likewise nods upon hearing what Julia has to propose. Although this type of analysis could look too detailed and fastidious, it allows us to see that *it is in the detail of interaction that the emergence of an organ can be identified.* Julia *proposes* a specific division of labor, which is *accepted* by both Joey and Patrick, with Joey playing the role of the representative or voice of this new subgroup. Everything thus happens as though the "you" she proposes was indeed becoming a "we," as far as Joey and Patrick are concerned. As insignificant as this could sound, it is in this kind of interactional moment that something like an organ and an organizational form can be considered created, established, or constituted.

Although nothing has been signed per se, what we are also observing here is nothing other than the establishment of a form of *verbal contract* that commits or engages the two parties (Julia on one side, and Joey and Patrick on the other). If one of these parties were not to do what is now expected from them, Julia, Joey, or Patrick could rightly refer to this specific moment in order to complain about a breach in what was agreed upon, echoing what **ethnomethodology** would call the *accountable character of our actions and conducts.* For instance, imagine that Patrick started to take care of something other than bringing the boxes to the truck; either Joey or Julia would then be entitled to remind him what it is that he agreed to do. Similarly, should Julia start to complain that Joey and Patrick were only taking care of the boxes, they could also remind her that it is what she asked them to do.

As we see, and this is something that **semiotics** helps us understand, humans are constantly producing things, in this case speech acts, that, once produced, can later and retroactively affect them. As you might remember, in the examples I used in chapter 2 to illustrate the semiotic perspective, I spoke about directories, call buttons, arrows, and logos, as well as pieces of furniture and decorations, which were all *doing things,* that is, participating in the organization of a building. But even something as evanescent and apparently ephemeral as a commitment or an agreement can later *act* or *do things* by *binding* the people who produced it to do what they agreed to do. This agreement sealed on line 4 indeed *commits* or *binds* the ones who reached it. In other words, communication is, as pointed out by Sigman (1995), consequential – that is, it *here and now* contributes to the production, instauration, or establishment of specific things that can *then later* have an important bearing on what is happening in the future.

We also observe that another double interact closes itself when Julia says, "Great," on line 6, implicitly marking that she acknowledges that both Joey and Patrick agreed with what she just proposed. An agreement, as mundane and insignificant as it might look, has now been reached and she can now switch to another organizational matter, to another organ, so to speak.

I previously noticed that the double interact that Joey initiated on line 1 ("OK, Julia, how do you think we should proceed?") could be considered only partially closed when both Patrick and Joey, on line 4, mark their agreement with what Julia proposed that they do. Why is it only partially closed? Because Julia's third friend, Amy, does not know yet how she should proceed. It is only when she knows what she could do that the double interact might be considered to be completed. Julia is then still responding to Joey's question when she proposes that Amy be in charge of "placing the boxes that Joey and Patrick will bring [her] to the back of the vehicle" (lines 7–8).

In keeping with **semiotics**, something like the question posed by Joey on line 1 continues to commit or bind Julia when she is telling Amy what she could do. As we begin to understand, communication thus is not a neutral endeavor to the extent that it (morally) commits, compels, or binds the people who are engaged in it. As noted by **conversation analysts** and **ethnomethodologists**, a question calls for a response (negative or positive), an invitation calls for an acceptance or a refusal, and even a simple statement (about the weather, for instance) calls for a reaction on the part of the person to whom this talk is addressed (Heritage, 1984).

This does not mean, of course, that a response will necessarily follow a question or that a reaction will necessarily follow a statement about the weather. However, it means that both a response and a reaction are considered to be *accountably due*. Imagine, for instance, that Julia willingly or unwillingly omits to propose to Amy what she could do; Amy could then justifiably ask, "What about me?," or be puzzled or even insulted by this lack of attention on Julia's part.

But this is not what happens – Julia proposes something to Amy – and we then see Amy accepting what Julia proposes ("That's fine with me," line 9), an acceptance that is then acknowledged by Julia ("OK," line 10). Another double interact ((1) Julia's proposal to Amy; (2) Amy's acceptance; (3) Julia's acknowledgment) can thus be considered as closed and completed. Another agreement has therefore been sealed, an agreement that, similarly to the previous one, commits the persons who reached it, here Amy and Julia – Amy because she agreed to place the boxes in the back of the vehicle, Julia because this is what she asked Amy to do and not something else, which means that Julia is also bound by what she told Amy.

In organizational terms, we also note that the question asked by Joey on line 1 can now be considered to be fully answered when Amy says, "That's fine with me," on line 9: Julia's three friends now know and agree with what Julia proposed they could/should do. This concern, initially raised by Joey on line 1, has now been addressed and resolved. They can proceed. The division of labor is now considered to be completed and people can indeed start to work.

Taylor and Van Every (2000) call the overlap of actions and activities of a person or a group of persons *imbrication, not unlike* the scales of a fish or the tiles of a roof. If we retrospectively look at what happened between Julia, Amy, Patrick, and Joey, we indeed saw how Julia first initiated a program of action: moving from her apartment, a program for which she decided to mobilize her three friends. Having agreed to participate, these latter need, of course, to know what to do in order to help Julia, which is what prompts Joey to ask his question on line 1.

Joey's question can thus be considered to be *imbricated* within Julia's general project of moving. But note that in responding to Joey's question, Julia likewise imbricates her own contribution to Joey's program of action: she tells her friends what they could do in order to help her, that is, she is addressing what their concern might be at this point. The imbrication does not stop here as we saw that in doing so, Julia imbricates her friends' future actions within specific programs of action, that is, she organizes their actions to come: Joey and Patrick will bring the boxes to the truck and Amy will place the boxes to the back of the vehicle. A division of labor has started to take place. *A body of friends has been given organs*. A system/organization is emerging.

Organizing, Subjection, and Authority

From a **critical** and **rhetorical** perspective, it is clear that organizing and coordination presuppose, by definition, forms of *subjection*. Although at first sight the example I chose appears rather neutral in terms of power and domination, it is noteworthy that the question of authority (and therefore power) is far from being absent, as we are now going to see.

Remember, for instance, that it is *Julia* who is asked by Joey to decide how they should proceed for the moving. In doing this, Joey thus implicitly positions Julia as the one who presumably has the authority or legitimacy necessary to tell the others what to do. Imagine, as a matter of contrast, that it was Amy who had initiated this division of labor. Chances are that the other movers might have found that unusual or inappropriate. Why? Precisely because they could consider that Amy does not have the authority to do so (except, of course, if her friends were to consider that she had some kind of expertise in this domain).[2]

As Taylor and Van Every (2000, 2011) remind us, author and authority have a common etymological root, *auctor*, a Latin word that means the father, the creator, the genitor, the one who initiates, protects, and sanctions. The person who is explicitly or implicitly positioned as having authority over specific affairs thus is the one who is by the same token positioned as the author of what will happen under his or her authority. And it is for this reason that this person will also usually be granted the power to sanction what is done "under her authority"; she will be able to evaluate what was done *for her*, that is, in her name.

So why is it Julia who is positioned by Joey as having the

authority to tell the others what to do? Because, in many ways, she previously positioned herself as the *initiator* of this whole enterprise: she is the one who decided to move from her apartment and she is the one who called her friends to ask for help. Implicitly, she is thus the *author* (the genitor, originator, instigator) of the moving to the extent that the three other persons are essentially positioned as her helpers or aides. As we see through this analysis, communicating thus automatically involves questions of power and authority, as it involves questions of authorship and responsibility (Taylor and Van Every, 2000).

This does not mean, of course, that this initial authority could not be redefined. For example, and as mentioned previously, Julia (or someone else in the group) could have positioned a person with more experience in moving as the one who is allowed to tell the others what to do. What matters at this point is to realize that authority, legitimacy, and power have a lot to do with *who* or even *what* is talking in a given situation (Cooren, 2010). For instance, when Julia is talking in the context of this move, it is also the-initiator-of-the-move who is talking. As we saw, this identity positions her as the main *author* of this whole program of action, hence her author-ity.

Similarly, if it were a person with some experience in moving who was talking, it would be not only he or she who was deemed to talk, but also his or her experience, an experience that would lend or give weight to what he or she was saying. If you find this type of analysis unusual (since it consists of saying that such a thing as "experience" is deemed to speak or say things in a given situation), just think of expressions like "experience speaks (for itself)," "experience speaks volumes," "experience speaks the truth," or "experience speaks louder." All these expressions show what *weight* we tend to attribute to experience in our daily life and the extent to which it can be deemed to indeed speak or express itself in specific circumstances (we will return to this point later in the book).

If we go back to the interaction, we can also see how such things as power and authority can be negotiated by the participants. For instance, note how Julia begins to respond to Joey's question by saying, "Well, I don't know," which amounts to marking the limit of her expertise and know-how in this situation. Some interactional work is thus done by Julia to avoid looking too authoritative or excessively directive. This positioning is confirmed by what she says just after (*"why don't you* and Patrick take care of bringing the boxes to the truck?,"* lines 2–3), an indirect speech act that positions her as *proposing* something to Joey and Patrick, and not as bluntly and directly telling them what to do.

This positioning is confirmed when she later turns to Amy while saying, *"would you mind* placing the boxes ... " (lines 6–8), which also consists of letting Amy decide whether or not she thinks what Julia proposes is a good idea. Finally, the same mitigation is expressed from lines 13 to 14 when Julia tells Patrick, "You *could* start with the boxes that are in the bedroom, *if it's okay with you*," another turn of talk that consists of positioning Julia as *proposing* something to Patrick and Joey (instead of, more straightforwardly, telling them what to do).

As we see through this analysis, authority is something that has to be enacted and performed on the terra firma of interaction (Benoit-Barné and Cooren, 2009). Although Julia is implicitly positioned by her friends' questions as the one who can tell them what to do, we also notice the **rhetorical** work she is doing not to look too directive or authoritative. She might be the author of the move, but everything happens as though she was also rhetorically positioning her friends as *co-authors* of this enterprise, so to speak. Joey, Patrick, and Amy are indeed co-authors to the extent that Julia implicitly asks them *what they think* about what she is proposing. In other words, the programs of action that she proposes or suggests are also *their* programs, not only because this is what they would be supposed to do, but also because they are positioned as *having a say* on what they should do.

If Joey, Patrick, and Amy are becoming *subjects*, in the critical and etymological sense of the term (i.e., they are subjected to someone else's program of action), we also see that some work is rhetorically done, especially by Julia, to make such a subjection look as smooth and acceptable as possible. If, as pointed out by Foucault, people cannot escape their condition of subject, even in situations that are apparently as innocuous and neutral as the friendly scenario we have been analyzing, some rhetorical work can be done to make this subjection more acceptable or tolerable, which is what Julia is doing here.

From a **critical perspective**, we could also note that even if this situation does not appear to be displaying signs of oppression or domination (after all, we are just talking about friends helping one of them move from her apartment!), it contributes to reproducing specific roles and responsibilities that could always be called into question. For instance, it is not by chance that Julia is asking Joey and Patrick to take care of the most physical part of the moving process (bringing the boxes to the truck) while she and Amy will respectively take care of packing the boxes and organizing them in the back of the truck.

Despite this division of labor seeming a priori innocuous, it tends to reproduce traditional ways of conceiving of gender identities, roles, and responsibilities (Ashcraft and Mumby, 2004). Although nobody in the group appears to question this division of labor (as Althusser points out, ideologies remain invisible to most of the people who are subjected to them), it is noteworthy that the four friends are de facto subjected to specific regimes of truth (Foucault's vocabulary) or ideologies (Althusser's terminology). What are these regimes of truth or ideologies – what could also be called "these orders of discourse"? As we already know, they are the presuppositions, assumptions, norms, rules, or beliefs that are supposed to distinguish what is considered to be true or right from what is considered to be false or wrong.

In this specific case, as innocuous as it seems to be, these regimes of truth or ideologies could be identified with the fact that it is *taken for granted, normal, typical,* or *presupposed* that men should take care of the tasks that are more physically demanding, while women should be in charge of tasks that are less physically challenging and/or more detail-oriented. The fact that Julia's proposal does not appear to be questioned by her friends confirms the ideological character of this division, given that it implies that this latter appears expected, reasonable, and unquestionable to them.

Note, as Foucault would say, that the point is not to necessarily question the reasonability, legitimacy, or validity of this division (after all, one could point out that this latter makes sense given that, on average, women tend to be less strong, physically speaking, than men), but to note that this division of labor is not neutral and is based on specific ways of conceiving of gender roles and capabilities. From a critical perspective, one could then notice that it is not only Julia, Amy, Joey, and Patrick who are expressing themselves in this specific interaction, but also specific ideologies, regimes of truth, or Discourses (with a big D). In other words, any interaction, however innocuous and innocent, can be considered the expression of specific ideologies, norms, or values (Wodak, 1999).

From a **rhetorical perspective**, one could also notice that this specific interaction amounts to *defining* or *constituting the situation* in a specific way and that this definition will, of course, reproduce specific ideologies, norms, or even truths to the detriment of others. How is this situation defined? Precisely by allocating or attributing specific roles, identities, and responsibilities to the persons present. As pointed out by rhetoric, communicating consists of implicitly or explicitly marking what matters or counts in a given situation, precisely what we see happening in this interaction.

By interacting the way they do, Julia, Amy, Joey, and Patrick indeed end up co-defining what matters or counts for them not only in terms of *what they want or intend to do* (moving Julia's apartment, being as effective as possible, etc.), but also in terms of *what makes them do what they do* (their presuppositions, belief systems, or ideologies). Rhetorically speaking, we could say that some specific values, norms, and interests thus end up being implicitly reaffirmed, expressed, and re-enacted through this interaction.

Narrating and Organizing

So far, we have seen what five of the six perspectives (i.e., rhetoric, semiotics, speech act theory, ethnomethodology, CDA) could tell us about coordinating and organizing, but no mention has been made of **narrative analysis**. Does that mean this perspective would have nothing to tell us about how people get organized, a phenomenon that appears so central to the organizational world? Indeed, at first sight, this absence looks understandable, given that no story is being told in the interaction just studied. Julia, Amy, Joey, and Patrick are not recounting events or anecdotes to each other; they are trying to agree how to coordinate their activities.

However, if we look at the interaction itself, we cannot but notice that it seems to display features that, in many respects, correspond with some of the ones that Bruner (1991) identified in narratives. In other words, what is happening between the four friends illustrates a distinction that some scholars have already proposed between what they call *stories told* and *stories lived* (Barge, 2004; Pearce and Pearce, 1998; Pearce, 1994). As Barge (2004) points out: "Stories lived refer to the details of our experiences and actions whereas stories told refer to the descriptions and interpretations that persons create regarding their lived experience" (p. 113). While Sam Steingerg's anecdote, in the previous chapter, would qualify as a story told, what happens between the four friends could be analyzed as a story lived, or as an antenarrative, that is, a sequence of actions that could later be retold by the protagonists themselves or by any person who had witnessed it.

Why can this sequence be analyzed like a narrative? Following similar features to those referred to by Bruner (1991), we could note that it displays the following: *diachronicity* (it is occurring over time); *particularity* (this move corresponds with specific events in specific circumstances); *intentional state entailment* (this sequence is characterized by events that concern its protagonists, i.e., they have a task to complete: moving); *hermeneutic composability* (this sequence is characterized by specific turns of talk that make sense because of their function or role in the deployment of the moving process); *genericness* (as ethnomethodologists would say, what happens can be recognized as a move because it displays typical or generic ways to do moving for another next first time); and *normativeness* (for instance, we saw that the distribution of labor presupposed specific norms, especially in terms of gender).

However, what seem to be missing in this account of a story

lived are *canonicity* and *breach* (no problem appears to occur during the interaction, i.e., there is no breach), and *referentiality* (since there is no breach, there is no side to be taken as to what might have triggered or caused this breach), as well as *context sensitivity* and *negotiability* (since it is not yet told but lived, there are no specific perspectives that can be negotiated). What explains the lack of characteristics is that, in many respects, this story lived is (let's face it!) quite boring and uneventful. No disagreement arises as to who should do what; no accidents occur, all of which means that no sides need be taken as to whom should be blamed.

But this absence of noteworthiness does not mean that narrativity has nothing to say about what happens in this situation. To illustrate that, I need to briefly introduce the work of another narratologist, Algirdas Julien Greimas (1983, 1987; Cooren, 2000; Taylor and Van Every, 2000) who also happened to be a semiotician. Greimas (1917–92) was originally a Lithuanian who spent the biggest part of his academic career in France, and was considered one of the most important figures of an intellectual movement called "structuralism." There is insufficient space here for an indepth look at his ideas and theory (for more details, see Bencherki and Cooren, 2011; Cooren, 2000; Robichaud, 2002, 2003; as well as Taylor and Cooren, 2006), but what matters to us is that Greimas was particularly interested in unveiling the basic structure of narratives (in this respect, he was greatly influenced by Claude Levi-Strauss (1963, 1973), a French anthropologist, and Vladimir Propp (1968), a Russian formalist).

As Greimas (1987) noted, narrative forms are characterized by several features, many of which echo Bruner's (1991) ideas. First, there must be some kind of breach, disorder, or problem, which is then supposed to trigger a program of action directed at re-establishing some kind of order or stability. Just imagine, for instance, a classical James Bond movie and you will have a picture of what Greimas has in mind.

In any James Bond narrative, at some point in the beginning there is always an event that is supposed to pose a threat to the order of the world: for instance, a nuclear weapon is stolen by a terrorist organization. Someone, let's call him a *mandator* – i.e., a person who defines a mandate or mission – then asks someone else, let's call him a *mandatee* (the one who receives the mandate), to respond to this defined threat. If he or she accepts the mission, this mandatee then becomes an *agent* acting for a *principal* (i.e., the person we initially called the mandator). Having accepted this *mandate* or *mission*, the agent will then perform a series of actions that are supposed to ultimately lead him or her to re-establish a new order. These actions will imply the mobilization of *helpers* and the foiling of *opponents*. At the end of this program of action, the mandator/principal can then evaluate the situation by recognizing whether or not the agent fulfilled the mission, which then leads him or her to reward or sanction the agent.

In a typical James Bond movie, you thus have the following distribution of roles:

- Mandator/principal = M.
- Mandatee/agent = James Bond.
- Mandate/Mission = Saving the world.
- Helpers = his gadgets, informers, aides, etc.
- Opponents = the terrorists, traitors, etc.

As Greimas points out (and this echoes Bruner's (1991) point on tellability), any narrative, in order to be interesting, needs to have a *polemical* dimension (see also Taylor and Van Every, 2000). A program of action thus needs to run against a sort of counterprogram, what Greimas calls an *anti-program*. People must disagree or fight about something. For example, in any James Bond movie, you usually have the arch-villain who acts as the anti-mandator/principal and initiates an anti-program of action against which James Bond is fighting. This arch-villain him or herself mandates an anti-agent who will be the main enemy of James Bond throughout the movie. It goes without saying that this anti-agent has his or her anti-helpers (who are James Bond's opponents) and his or her anti-opponents (James Bond himself, as well this latter's helpers).

Interestingly, Greimas also identifies that any narrative is marked by a hierarchy of actions. As noticed before, the mandator/principal is the person who not only initiates the program of action, but also evaluates its completion at the end. In the case of a James Bond movie, it is M who initiates the mission, but also typically rewards, recognizes, or congratulates James Bond for fulfilling the mission. All the events that take place between the giving of the mission and its recognition, evaluation, or sanction will therefore be considered *subsumed*, *imbricated*, or *embedded* within this program. Thus, any main program of action itself includes several sub-programs of action.

This explains why the use of Greimas's narratology is especially interesting to understand organizing, since it allows us to show that this type of activity implies, by definition, that some programs of action be imbricated in or subsumed to others. In order to illustrate this point, let us return to our initial illustration: Julia's moving. Although the interaction between the friends definitely has a linear dimension (they are speaking one after another and their respective contributions follow each other), Greimas helps us recognize that this linearity hides, in fact, several imbrications, that is, overlapping and embedded moves, which constitute the building blocks of organizing.

For example, we could note that the whole process of moving started because Julia decided to move to a new apartment. In the story, we do not know why she decided to do that, but we could imagine that she wants to move because her apartment is too small. Although we are far from the type of breach in a James Bond film, where nuclear weapons are stolen, we can notice that the whole program of action – moving – is initiated because of some kind of problem or disorder that needs to be solved or addressed: her apartment is too small, therefore she wants/needs to move to a bigger one.

We saw that, having decided to move, Julia then decides to enlist the help of three of her friends – Joey, Patrick, and Amy – by asking them to join her on a specific day. "Mandator" might be too strong a word in this case, but we see that Julia acts as the person who *initiates* the whole program of action: moving her apartment. And chances are that she will also be the one who, by definition, will *close* it when she thanks her friends at the end (at least, this would be expected from her friends and should she neglect to do so, she could be directly criticized or at least the object of reproach). All the activities between these two moments will *make sense* because they are narratively subsumed to or imbricated in this program that she initiated (Browning and Weick, 1986; Robichaud, 2001, 2002, 2003).

In this specific case, we also see that Julia not only acts as the mandator/initiator, but also as one of the agents, given that she will act in the team that is moving her apartment. Greimas indeed notes that actors can have many roles in a narrative, which means that nothing prevents someone from mandating himself or herself. In this case, we also see the creation of a *collective agent*, a "we" created by the program of action she proposed to Joey, Patrick, and Amy. This collective agent, consisting of Julia, Joey, Patrick, and Amy is *acting for* Julia, who is the principal.

This position of principal is confirmed when we see Julia not only being asked what they should do ("OK, Julia, how do you think we should proceed?," line 1), but also telling the other friends what to do (lines 2–3, lines 6–7, lines 13–14). She is thus identified by the others as the principal, but she also acts *as such* by telling her friends what should be done. The division of labor is therefore something that Julia creates when she allocates various responsibilities to her friends, as we see from lines 1 to 17. If we had to represent how this organizing is taking place, we could use figure 3.1.

As we see, organizing thus also consist in creating programs of action that are going to supersede others. But what is especially important to retain is that this embedding and subsuming has to be *interactively achieved*. If Julia's moving plan can progress, it is because she and her friends initiate some moves that are going to contribute to its completion. Each phase of the program can potentially become problematic and lead to crisis. In our illustration, the narrative is kind of boring and eventless precisely because there is no breach, no violation, no problem, no interruption. The only problem is what triggers the whole activity, which is that Julia needs to move because her apartment is too small.

Following Taylor and Van Every (2000, 2011), we then see how organizing is mainly a matter of co-orientation by which people

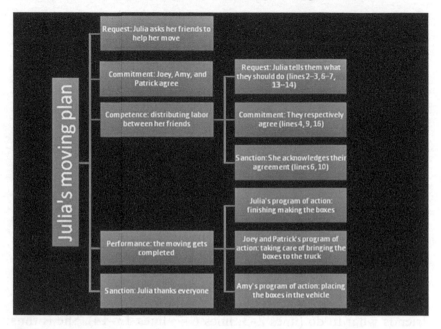

Figure 3.1 Julia's moving from a narrative perspective

interactionally orient to a common object(ive), creating imbrications between various sequences of action. But what we also see is that any form of collective organizing also implies a *distribution of sub-objectives (or sub-orientations)*, which correspond with the various sub-programs of action – what we previously called the organs – that are established and enacted. While Julia is finishing making the boxes, Joey and Patrick are in charge of taking the boxes to the truck, so that Amy can place them in the vehicle. If the four friends are ideally co-oriented to the same objective (moving Julia's possessions to a new apartment), they are also – each of them – oriented to different tasks/programs of action that are supposed to articulate with each other.

If such a distribution is what characterizes organizing, it is also one of its weakest points in that participants might start to exclusively focus on their respective tasks, responsibilities, or submissions while somehow forgetting or neglecting the main mission or objective. As pointed out by Latour (2013), people might also quarrel about their respective responsibilities or duties, a situation that pervades the organizational world, as we know: "This is your responsibility, not mine!" or "Why are you doing that? This is my job!" (see also Bencherki and Cooren, 2011).

Although the example I chose to illustrate organizing appears somewhat pre-organizational (to the extent that the team formed by Julia, Joey, Patrick, and Amy does not qualify as an established organization with a formal distribution of titles and responsibilities), we see that it already contains the seed of any kind of organizational situation. As soon as responsibilities, authorities, and tasks are defined and allocated (something that is established, as we saw, through specific **speech acts**), people will be attached to them, creating the conditions for conflicts and clashes if these programs of action come to contradict or conflict with each other, which often happens in formal organizations.

Should we have a formal organization (e.g., a removal company), Julia might be the leader of the team, while Joey, Patrick, and Amy would be her subordinates, each of them having specific responsibilities, titles, and tasks to be fulfilled. In addition, hiring contracts would have to be signed, with specific policies followed, schedules and budgets respected, salaries paid, and so on. Organizing would still be taking place, but with more constraints and resources (Giddens, 1979; McPhee and Zaug, 2000).

As pointed out by the **semiotic** perspective, titles, job descriptions, contracts, policies, schedules, budgets, and salaries would then become the *co-authors* of the moving experience. Why co-authors? Because they would literally contribute to the organizing process per se. For instance, it would be *in the name of* the salary they receive and the contract that *binds* them to their company that Joey, Patrick, and Amy would move the contents of apartments and houses *for* the organization that employs them. Similarly, they could *invoke* specific policies, job descriptions, or schedules to enjoin their boss to respect some of their decisions or rights, and their boss could, of course, do the same (Benoit-Barné and Cooren, 2009). By invoking them, they would make these policies, budgets, and schedules *say something*, which means that these policies and schedules would be presented as *authorizing*, *authoring*, or *dictating* specific actions or decisions.

As we see, there is no paradigmatic change when we switch from an informal organization (a bunch of pals moving the contents of an apartment) to a formal one (a removal company). What we see, however, is that some specific agents (policies, job descriptions, contracts, schedules, titles, organizational charts, etc.) start to matter or count because they can be invoked by the human participants, that is, people can start to make them say things in a given interaction in order to defend a position or enjoin others to do something they would not have done otherwise. A formal organization, as implied in the name, is *an organization with specific forms*, that is, specific agents or figures (a figure is a form) that have the specificity to endure and last, giving to the organization not only its form(s), but also its capacity to remain and perpetuate itself.

As you might remember, this is what **semiotics** helps us recognize. An organization is not only made of human beings, but also of other (non-human) agents that, in many respects, define its mode of existence and courses of action. People come and go (are hired and fired), but titles, organizational charts, functions, missions, and so on remain (although these latter can, of course, also be replaced and changed) and contribute to organizing by dictating specific courses of action. The key point to remember, however, is that there is no harmonizing force (Tarde, 1895/2012) that can ensure that all these agencies (human and non-human) will coherently and consistently work with each other.

If there seems to be an organizational *system*, it is because of all the technologies, titles, job descriptions, charts, and units that iteratively and systematically define what needs to be done or what courses of action need to be taken. From a critical viewpoint, however, these imbrications presuppose effects of subordination and submission, but also of resistance and subversion (Knights, 2002; Knights and Willmott, 1989). We will explore all these questions in the following chapters.

4

Organizational Culture, Identity,
and Ideology

Now that we have tackled the organizing properties of discourse, consider three important aspects of organizational life – namely culture, identity, and ideology – to show what role discourse might play in their constitution. Why these three topics altogether? Generally, it is hard to speak about one without addressing the others. When you contact with organization, you soon discover that there are specific values, norms, artifacts, or practices that tend to characterize it, defining what we usually call its identity and culture. If, in addition, you start thinking critically about this organization, you then realize that this culture and identity also convey specific ideologies which might not be specific to this collective, but which could be representative of certain interests – usually managerial – to the detriment of others (Deetz, 1992; Knights, 2002).

In what follows, I will thus show you what our six perspectives can tell us about organizational culture, identity, and ideology, keeping in mind that the point of this book is to provide specific analytical methods to support the study of organizations from a discursive perspective. But before doing that, let us first see what we mean by culture and identity (the question of ideology having already been addressed in chapter 2).

Culture and Identity

As Alvesson (2004) reminds us, the term "organizational culture" can mean many different things, depending on who is studying it. As he points out, "a glance at just a few works that use the term 'organizational culture' will reveal enormous variation in the definitions of this term and even more in the use of the term 'culture'" (p. 318). In other words, we all have a vague intuition about what an organizational culture might be or look like, but problems seem to emerge when attempting to define what it is or consists of (Martin, 1992, 2001; Van Maanen, 2011). This, in itself, should not be too surprising as defining consists of (somewhat arbitrarily) delineating an object of study, something people often resist, and for good reasons (Deetz, 2001).

One solution, as previously proposed in chapter 1, is to start not from a technical definition of the word, but from its general usage and etymology. By relying on a common-sense definition of the word "culture," we avoid an unending debate about what might be its *proper* definition. The advantage of a common-sense definition is indeed that it does not belong a priori to anyone – in other words, it is not supposed to be proper to a specific viewpoint, author, or approach – and it reflects what people tend to mean (or historically meant) when using this terminology.

Etymologically, we could thus start by noticing that "cultivating" comes from the Latin *cultivare*, which means plowing, harrowing, or tilling. This word was originally used to speak about what we do to a land when trying to grow something, a definition of the word that still exists today, whether in English, French, or Spanish, just to name a few languages. It was only in the seventeenth century that a more figurative sense started to emerge, conveying the idea of "improving by training or education." As for the word "culture" in itself, its origins are, of course, similar: the Latin word *cultura* literally means "agriculture" and, more figuratively, "care" and "honoring" – which gave, for instance, the word "cult."

As we see, the words "cultivate" and "culture" thus imply the idea of making something grow, evolve, mature, improve, or maintain itself. While people originally used this word to convey the idea of growing crops on a land, they began using this terminology to also speak about other things they were taking care of, maintaining, sustaining, or perpetuating throughout their activities. From the cultivation of carrots, lettuces, and wheat, we thus passed to the cultivation of habits, ways of speaking, values, norms, and styles!

This detour through etymology allows us to understand why it seems so difficult for scholars to agree on a definition of the word "culture," given that it can etymologically mean *anything* that could be the object of a form of maintenance, upholding, and perpetuation. For instance, Clifford Geertz (1973), a famous anthropologist, considers that culture is "an historically transmitted pattern of *meanings* embodied in symbols, a system of inherited *conceptions* expressed in symbolic forms by means of which men communicate, perpetuate, and develop their knowledge about and their attitudes toward life" (p. 89; my italics).

His definition therefore focuses on transmission, perpetuation, and inheritance of meanings and conceptions in connection with people's knowledge and attitudes. His view of culture thus seems at least partly coherent with the etymology and common-sense definition of the word. Cultivating a given conception of the world can indeed amount to transmitting it to others, who then inherit it so that this conception can perpetuate itself throughout generations. However, other things could also be considered to be transmitted, sustained, and inherited: a specific *technique* that a group of people use to produce artifacts, a *ritual* that they keep re-enacting on a regular basis, or certain *values* that they appear to cherish, be attached to and reproduce. Focusing on meaning alone thus appears a little too reductive (Eisenberg and Riley, 2001); there are other things at play.

Furthermore, while scholars who study culture tend to define it in terms of what is *shared* among cultural members (Martin, 2001: 16), an etymological and commonsensical approach invites us to focus on what is *cultivated* in a given group, community, organization, or society (Cooren, 2010; Cooren et al., 2013). Although this conception – a culture corresponds with anything that is cultivated

– could be considered tautological, the tautology actually disappears when we replace the verb "cultivating" with its synonyms: perpetuating, maintaining, nurturing, sustaining, etc., which show that a given culture is the (logical) result of specific activities that maintain and perpetuate its existence throughout time and space.

Interestingly, this conception allows us to develop a *performative* and *constitutive* view of culture, given that this latter becomes the result or product of specific actions, activities, and practices. *In order to be and exist, a specific culture thus has, by definition, to be perpetuated and sustained through people's conversations, texts, and practices in general* (Van Maanen, 2011). We will see later why such a conception proves to be especially interesting for scholars interested in discourse analysis.

But let us now focus on "identity," another term that is widely used and discussed in social sciences and humanities, and has strong ties with the idea of culture (Hatch and Schultz, 1997). In keeping with our approach, we could first look at the etymology of the term, an approach that again departs from the literature that tends to identify it as a theoretical (and thus technical) construct (see, for instance, Albert and Whetten, 1985; Whetten, 2006). Identity comes from the Latin *idem*, which means "the same" and the Latin suffix *itas*, which means "the state, condition or quality of being something." Etymologically speaking, "identity" therefore means the state, condition, or quality of being the same, which could also be defined as sameness or likeness.

When we speak of the identity of something or someone, we thus refer to what appears to *characterize* this thing or person, that is, specific traits, qualities, or attributes that are supposed to define what this thing or person is or supposed to be – what makes it, him, or her, be or look the same *throughout time and space*. As the philosopher Derrida (1988) and other scholars like Garfinkel (2002), Tarde (1895/2012) or Latour (2013) have noticed, sameness, however, implies otherness to the extent that being or remaining the same also presupposes an evolution, alteration, or development in time and space.

Even if things and persons, of course, differ, evolve, and change *in some aspects* throughout time and space (they get older, they move in one direction or another, they alter themselves, etc.), some other aspects, qualities, or attributes that characterize these things and persons can (appear to) remain or be defined as being the same. Although this reflection could be considered too philosophical and abstract, I would like to show you that it actually resonates with some basic aspects of our mundane experience.

Nobody will, for instance, deny that something like a nationality can be an important aspect of someone's identity (even if that is far from being always the case). Although someone might change or evolve in several aspects (by getting different jobs and responsibilities throughout her life, by acquiring new skills and abilities, by getting married or divorced, etc.), her nationality might remain *the same* throughout her life (although this does not have to be the case). Usually, this identity was legally defined when the person was born because of her birthplace or her parents' nationality. Here, we see that something like (an) identity can, in some cases, be institutionally ascribed to people without them having anything to say about it.

Even if the question of identity might, at first sight, look quite complex, we see that, practically speaking, it can also be a non-issue for some of its aspects (for instance, someone could say, "I'm American, what's the problem?"). However, identity can also be contested, challenged, or disputed when discussions, negotiations, or even fights occur about what someone or something is. Identity can also be the object of particular attention when, for example, a person or an organization (through one of its representatives) wants to project a specific image of what she, he, or it is. And this is where the detailed study of discourse and interaction can become very interesting.

This development also brings us to the connection between identity and culture, a connection that is, as we will see, not necessarily automatic. Some identities indeed are not necessarily cultivated. For instance, you could be technically Canadian because your mother was born in Canada and gave you this nationality when you were born, but this identity could then be reduced to an official document that would certify this identity (an interesting case of textual agency that will be examined later), but would play no role in your daily life.

However, being Canadian, as an identity, could be cultivated, should you invoke it in your conversations or should your inter-locutors refer to it when talking to you (especially if you happen not to live in Canada). An identity does not have to be cultivated in order to exist (someone could be technically Canadian without making this identity an important part of her life or conversa-tions), but it starts to be especially significant when it becomes the object of negotiation, debate, or invocation in a given discussion or text.

As we begin to realize, studying what is cultivated in a conversa-tion or in various texts and documents can thus lead to a reflection on identity. For instance, cultivating specific values, norms, or principles indeed means that these values, norms, or principles will be implicitly or explicitly nurtured, sustained, and perpetuated in people's talk, marking a form of attachment on their part, an attachment that they or others could relate to their identity. Paying attention to culture and identity from a discursive perspective thus consists of analyzing what tends to *repeatedly lead people to say what they say or do what they do*. It is in this repetition and cul-tivation of the *same* values, norms, and principles that something like an identity can sometimes be affirmed or recognized.

Unfolding Organizational Identities from Discourse

So far, we have addressed the question of culture and identity in very general terms, and I have been careful not to imply that I was only speaking, say, about organizational culture or individual identity. For example, what I have written about identity could certainly be applied to the identity of a person (we saw this with the question of nationality), but could also be said of *anything* people would be implicitly or explicitly identifying or invoking in a given discussion, debate, or conversation: an organization, an artifact, an idea, etc. The same reasoning applies for the notion of culture as what I have written about cultivation, and cultivating does not have to be reduced to the question of organizational culture, but could also be extended to groups, teams, families, institutions, or societies in general.

But since this book is devoted to organizational discourse, I will now focus on what our six perspectives can tell us about organizational cultures and identities (adding, of course, the key question of ideologies). At this point, you may notice that I am using the *plural* form, since I certainly do not want to convey a monolithic view on these issues. As you might remember from chapter 3, organizations are characterized by a distribution of tasks, authorities, and responsibilities, which means that, by definition, members will end up cultivating or perpetuating various cultures, identities, and ideologies, depending on what their tasks, authorities, and responsibilities are, especially in large organizations.

This does not rule out the existence of *an* organizational culture, identity, and ideology (without an s/singular) – that is, some specific values, principles, or habits, for instance, that might be characteristic of an organization as a whole (and that would be encouraged and sustained by the managerial team, for instance) – but organizations are, as we saw, also marked by their differentiation or even fragmentation, which irremediably leads to a differentiation and fragmentation of their cultures, identities, and ideologies (Martin, 1992, 2001).[1]

For instance, organizations are often characterized by their various communities of practice (Lave and Wenger, 1991; Wenger, McDermott, and Snyder, 2002), that is, communities of people representing not only certain professions, skills, or expertise, but also certain interests, concerns, and preoccupations. Just think of a hospital and you will have an idea of what I mean. Certain values, norms, or practices might be representative of a hospital as a whole because they appear to be cultivated and encouraged at all levels of the organization. However, because of its differentiation and fragmentation, a hospital will typically be characterized by various cultures, identities, and even ideologies, depending on the professions you decide to focus on: nurses, physicians, administrative staff, technicians, dieticians, and so on.

So what does this mean for people interested in organizational discourse? Simply that one of the ways (not, of course, *the* way) to study culture amounts to analyzing what is cultivated in people's conversations, texts, and practices in general, giving to these notions a performative and interactional twist, as mentioned earlier. Depending on the various norms, values, practices, identities, or ideas cultivated, an organization can thus be conceived as a polyphonic or plurivocal entity (Grant et al., 2004) where many different voices representing various cultures and identities can be heard, even if some tend to *count* more than others (Deetz, 1992).

So let us begin with identity and see what our perspectives can say about this issue. We could first notice that **speech act theory** appears well equipped to deal with this question. As pointed out in chapter 2, this perspective indeed highlights the *transformative* dimension of language, that is, the fact that in speaking, writing, and more generally communicating, people do not only inform each other, but also *transform* the world in some aspects. Obviously, some transformations happen to count more than others and we will especially focus on the ones that appear to matter the most.

For instance, if someone asks me to pass him a file, could we say that my identity is somewhat changed because I was asked to do something? I certainly have a new attribute (I *was* or *have* been asked to do something), but chances are that this might be completely inconsequential regarding my identity in the long term. But imagine other examples like "being appointed vice-president," "being demoted," "being hired," or "being fired" and you will understand what I mean when I say that some speech acts can count or matter more than others.

What speech act theorists call *declarations* (see chapter 2) are, for instance, the performatives par excellence precisely because they tend to change or transform people's identity in the long term (as we saw, identity implies the repetition of the same and a certain form of continuity): promoting, naming, condemning, and so on. Incidentally, this is why their production tends to be controlled, as we saw with the wedding illustration in chapter 2 (it must be the *right persons* with the *right words* in the *right circumstances*). For example, whoever wants to become an engineer or a physician will have to undergo a long educational process strewn with obstacles, a process that will be punctuated by a university delivering a diploma that will attest the new identity (engineer, physician) and its related expertise, rights, and responsibilities for the upcoming years.

According to speech act theory, something like an identity can thus be *objectified* or *reified* in a variety of documents that are supposed to *prove, guarantee,* or *attest* it. Even something like gender is, as we know, legally defined (usually through the definition of the child's sex – usually by an authorized person such as a physician – at his or her birth). I could multiply the examples that show what importance certain documents (passports, diplomas, birth certificates, hiring contracts, etc.) can thus have in our daily life, even if their contribution – that is, what they literally do – tends to be hidden or taken for granted (for more details, see Cooren, 2004).

But what this theory also reminds us – and this is crucial for people interested in discourse analysis – is that *specific speech acts oftentimes come with specific identities.* As Taylor and Van Every (2000, 2011) point out, some speech acts not only require, but also reaffirm, certain types of authority, which irremediably come with certain types of identity. I am not only speaking about obvious cases like "prescribing medicine to a patient" or "giving an order to someone," which respectively require and reaffirm the identity of physician and hierarchical authority. I am also speaking about cases where identities are not necessarily institutionally defined – that is, defined by official *titles* that are themselves certified by official documents like diplomas or hiring contracts – but can be affirmed, recognized, and attributed *in interaction.*

For instance, Barker (1999) proposed a very nice analysis of a self-management team in a company that he fictitiously called ISE communications. Self-management teams are especially interesting because they are designed as peer groups, usually comprising 10 to 15 employees, where no one is supposed to have a formal authority over the others. As he points out:

Self-managing workers assume for themselves much of the former tasks of the old supervisor. Instead of being told what to do by a supervisor, self-managing workers must gather and synthesize information, act on it, and take collective responsibility for those actions. (p. 5)

However, what Barker nicely shows through his ethnographic analyses is that this ideal portrait of a peer group managing itself is not without its dark side, so to speak.

Over time, workers develop "concertive control" (Barker, 1993), that is, a form of control where workers *concert with each other* to define how things should be done in this kind of team. He also shows how these self-management teams end up defining the values that matter or count to them, values that progressively transform themselves into norms and rules, which eventually become formalized as official policies for the team.

What remains to be shown, however, is how this is happening on the terra firma of interaction, which is where the study of organizational discourse can become quite interesting. Let us look, for instance, at the following situation, as described by Barker (1999):

In June 1991, the red team was experiencing a problem with one of its temporary workers, Phil. In the last week, Phil had become romantically involved with Sandy, who worked on the white team. Consequently, Phil had been finding excuses for going into the white team's area, for lingering at Sandy's workstation during breaks and lunches. In the last few days, a team member had had to go fetch him from the white team's area and remind him that the team had work to do. Phil had made the mistake of "resisting" the team's value consensus, and as Martha, the red team's coordinator at that time, told me later, "We just couldn't let it go. We had to take action before he got himself into trouble." Martha saw that Phil was late, again, getting back to work from a break. She got up from her work on testing, said something to Marty and Diego, two longer-tenured workers on the team, and went to the white team's area. She caught Phil's attention and beckoned him to come. She waited for him just behind the red team's area. Marty and Diego joined her. I was off to one side but still within hearing range. (p. 80)

Here is the transcript of their conversation, as reconstructed from Barker's notes:

1	Phil:	I was just coming back. It's not a big deal.
2	Martha	Look, Phil, we don't like the pattern you're setting here. You've
3		been late getting back and you're going to get yourself in trouble.
4	Phil	XX[X–
5	Martha	[You're a member of our team. We expect you to support all of
6		us. When we start back to work you have to be here. You can't be
7		hanging back.
8	Diego	You've got to support us. We all support each other. When you're
9		late, the rest of us have to work harder.
10	Martha:	That's not fair for any of us.
11	Phil	Now look=
12	Martha	=No, you look. This is a bad pattern you have going here. When you
13		work, you do a good job. But if you are not going to do what we
14		need you to do, if you are going to cause problems for the rest of us,
15		then we will have to do something. Don't make us do that.
16	Phil	((Phil looked at them)) OK OK.
17	Martha	We don't care about your personal life, what you do on your own
18		time. We don't mind you visiting Sandy every now and then. But
19		you've started to cause problems. We're worried that we can't
20		depend on you.
21	Diego	You're part of the team. You have to support us when we're at
22		work. Outside of work, you can do what you want.
23	Martha	Do you understand us? ((looking at Phil directly))
24	Phil	Yes, I understand. I'll watch myself more. I'm OK.
25		((Martha, Marty and Diego nodded and the meeting broke up))

(transcript reconstructed from Barker, 1999: 80–1)

So what do we see happening in this conversation? Of course, we could first notice that it is not by chance if it is Martha who takes the initiative to talk to Phil. Even if the self-management team is supposed to be a *peer* group, which would presuppose that everybody is a priori equal, some members appear to be, paraphrasing George Orwell (1945), *more equal than others*. Barker (1999) indeed mentions that Martha is the team's coordinator, a title that could be considered a flagrant contradiction within the peer philosophy of a self-management team. When she is talking in this excerpt, it is also the team coordinator who is talking, reprimanding Phil for what is presented as his misconduct. In other words, as a sort of team leader, she could definitely feel *authorized* to speak in the name of the team and her peers.

But let us look specifically at the various **speech acts** she is producing in this short interaction. For now, we will just focus on what she tells Phil and not on what Diego, one of her colleagues, is also saying. Marty, the other colleague she asked to join her, is not saying a word, but this does not mean that his presence does not make a difference. So, if we look at her speech acts, we could note that she is:

- *Telling Phil twice to pay attention to what she is about to say*: "Look" (line 2); "No, you look" (line 12).
- *Criticizing/reprimanding Phil*: "we don't like the pattern you're setting here. You've been late getting back" (lines 2–3); "This is a bad pattern you have going here" (line 12); "But you've started to cause problems" (line 20).
- *Warning/threatening Phil*: "you're going to get yourself in trouble" (line 3); "When you work you do a good job. But if you are not going to do what we need you to do, if you are going to cause problems for the rest of us, then we will have to do something. Don't make us do that." (lines 12–16).
- *Reminding Phil who he is*: "you're a member of our team" (line 5).
- *Reminding/telling Phil what their expectations are*: "We expect you to support all of us" (lines 5–6).
- *Telling/reminding him what he has to and cannot do*: "When we start back to work you have to be here. You can't be hanging back" (lines 6–7).
- *Telling Phil what his misconduct means for the group*: "That's not fair for any of us" ((line 10).
- *Interrupting him* (lines 5, 12).
- *Telling Phil how they feel about the situation*: "We don't care about your personal life, what you do on your own time. We don't mind you visiting Sandy every now and then" (lines 18–20); "We're worried that we can't depend on you" (lines 20–1).

- *Asking him if he fully understood what their move meant* (which could also be understood, of course, as a last warning): "Do you understand us?" (line 24).

Interestingly, we see that all these speech acts implicitly reaffirm Martha's authority over Phil and therefore her identity as a group coordinator and team leader. In other words, it is not enough to know, as noticed before, that she has the title of group coordinator (a title that was granted to her by her peers); *her interventions must reaffirm, enact, or confirm this identity*. What allows me to say that? Simply that criticizing/reprimanding Phil or warning/threatening him is not something that *any* member could a priori do.

Had one of his peers dared to do that, chances are that Phil would have responded, "Who are you to tell me that?" Note that Phil never questions Martha's authority to reprimand him, which means that, interactionally speaking, his responses somehow confirm, de facto, her right or authority to chastize or discipline him (and therefore her identity as a team leader). What he manages to do is simply minimize the problematic character of what he did (line 1), try to defend himself, while being interrupted by his interlocutors twice (lines 4 and 11), and finally acknowledge that he indeed made a mistake by promising that he will not do it again (lines 17 and 25). As **conversation analysts** would point out, this link of authority between Martha and Phil is thus not only reaffirmed by Martha herself, but also implicitly *confirmed* by Phil when he does not question her right to say what she is saying. In other words, it is *co-constructed* by these two participants, even if one participant – Phil – definitely appears to be subjected to the other's – Martha's – critiques and reprimands.

But note also how Martha is repeatedly talking on behalf of a "we" and an "us," which could be representing either Diego, Marty, and herself, but also and especially the self-managing team itself (lines 2, 5–6, 14, 18–21, and 24). Martha and her two colleagues are positioning themselves as *representing* the team, when they come to talk to Phil. Speaking on behalf of a "we" or "us" is thus another way by which she reaffirms her identity of group coordinator, an identity that, in return, authorizes her to speak to Phil the way she does. As already noticed, it is thus not only Martha who is speaking in this excerpt, but also the group coordinator, an identity/authority that is actualized and confirmed throughout the pronouns she is using in this interaction.

But we could go further and notice that when Martha is speaking for a "we" and an "us," it is as though it were the self-managing team itself that was also speaking. This move is important to recognize because we are not simply speaking about *people* talking to each other here, but also of *a group that is somehow talking to one of its members*. As Taylor and Van Every (2000) already noticed, *any* collective (a group, an organization, a society, etc.) needs a *voice* in order to exist and be recognized as such (see also Taylor and Cooren, 1997). In other words, the voice of a group contributes to the shaping and reaffirmation of its identity.

At first sight, you could reply that this is just a way of speaking and that the team does not really speak, only humans do (see, for instance, McPhee, 2004; McPhee and Iverson, 2009). But remember what **semiotics** taught us, which is that "telling things" or "doing things with words" is not the sole prerogative of human beings. In other words, we have to take seriously the fact that speaking *in the name of* a collective (an organization, a society, a group, a team, etc.), and being explicitly or implicitly recognized as authorized to do so, means that, automatically, it is this collective that also speaks through this person.

This is why, as noticed by Taylor and Van Every (2000), we can read in the newspapers that Apple *announced* the launching of a new version of its iPad or that Russia *condemned* a terrorist attack to UN representatives. Of course, *people* have to voice what an organization, a country, or a group thinks, wants, or says (these people are usually called *spokespersons*), but we have to take seriously these effects of representation, which adds to the *weight*, *force*, or even *power* of what the person is saying, that is, her authority.

Regarding what is happening in this interaction, we could thus notice that these effects of representation or delegation are defined not only by Martha's title of group coordinator (as the team coordinator, she is a priori authorized to speak in the name of the team, that is, in some circumstances, she can represent its interests, preoccupations, and voice), but also, as already noticed, by the pronouns she is using (we, us), which reaffirm *what the team* as a whole and its members are supposed to *think* of Phil's conduct.

For what concerns us, that is, the question of identity, this is quite significant, since it shows how the identity of a *team* can be enacted in what its delegates say and do in specific circumstances. Indeed, by warning Phil about what the team does not like in his behavior ("been late getting back," line 3, the fact that they "can't depend on [him]," lines 20–1) and expects regarding his future conduct ("to support all of us," lines 5–6), Martha is, in fact, also speaking *in the name of* her team's values, the values that, in many respects, are supposed to define her team's identity.

What are these values, as implicitly displayed in her reprimands, to which we could add her colleague Diego's, who also intervenes? To respond to this question, we need, as discourse analysts, to *unfold* them from what she is saying to Phil, that is, precisely answer the following question: *in the name of what kind of values is she speaking to Phil?* This might look complicated, but it is not, as I will show you now. For instance, when she tells Phil, "You're a member of our team. We expect you to support all of us. When we start back to work you have to be here. You can't be hanging back" (lines 5–7), you could reconstruct the value she is defending by noticing that she appears to be speaking in the name of a form of solidarity, cohesion, or even responsibility.

The ideas of solidarity, cohesion, or responsibility, as values, indeed imply and dictate that people help each other because they feel that they are part of a whole that they participate in, which is exactly what Martha is reminding Phil at this point. Although she never explicitly uses the terms *solidarity, cohesion, and responsibility* in her intervention, these are *values* that she is *implicitly* defending in this situation, values that incidentally are supposed to define and distinguish what self-managing teams are supposed to be all about (Barker, 1999). Because team members have the responsibility to manage their own teams, they are supposed to stand by and help each other, which is what solidarity and cohesion are all about.

In connection with the distinction between small d discourse vs. big D Discourse (see chapter 1), we also see how Martha is drawing from what could be called a *self-managing team Discourse*, comprised of specific terminologies ("team," "member," "support") and habitual forms of arguments ("You can't be hanging back"). This shows that we, as analysts, can be interested in the eventful character of conversation, that is, in what people are up to when they communicate with each other (small d discourse), while focusing on the repetition, reproduction, or iteration of specific topics of discussion, styles of communication, and rights to speak (big D Discourse).

Note also how Diego echoes her intervention when he adds, "You've got to support us. We all support each other. When you're late, the rest of us have to work harder" (lines 8–9). In terms of speech acts, he is: (1) telling Phil what he is supposed to do (i.e., support the other team members); (2) reminding him what the team members do or are supposed to do (i.e., support each other); and (3) telling him what consequences his conduct has on the other team members (i.e., they have to work harder).

Again, if we do the exercise of translating or analyzing what Diego is saying in terms of what *values* he is implicitly putting forward and defending, we can note that he also appears to be speaking in the name of a form of solidarity, which implies the idea of supporting each other, to which we could add the value of *equity* or *justice* (when he is telling Phil that his conduct forces other team members to work harder, which is a way to implicitly convey the unfair, inequitable, or unjust character of the situation). Again, the words "solidarity" and "equity" are never spelled out in this intervention, but they can be *reconstructed, unfolded,* and *identified* by our analyses.

Incidentally, we can also imagine that Barker (1999) reproduced this situation because this latter was, for him, representative of what self-management team members could say and do to each other in this company, which also means that it was representative of who they *were* and what the team *was* at that point. As we start to understand, a team identity or a team member identity comes with the enactment of specific values, norms, or principles *over a specific period of time*, marking the effect of continuity or stability that any identity requires.

Studying identity from a discursive perspective thus requires that you unfold or unveil what values, norms, and principles that speakers and writers implicitly refer to and mobilize in their turn of talk or texts, *for another next first time*. Something *implicit* indeed etymologically refers to something that is folded into something else (*plicare* means "to fold" in Latin). It is usually this *thing* that is folded into people's texts and turns of talk that will define their identity (whether individual or collective) because it is *what* will appear to continuously motivate what they say, marking their identity, that is, the identical character of what they say, do, and are.

Unfolding Organizational Cultures from Discourse

As I said earlier, some identities do not have to be cultivated in order to exist, but most of the time they are and this is why we can recognize them in a series of texts or conversations. If, for instance, solidarity and equity are key cultural traits for self-management teams, it means that they will, by definition, be *cultivated* through not only what their members say and do, but also the texts and documents they will promote or mobilize, or even the artifacts, objects, and decorations they will display.

As **semiotics** reminds us, all these things, texts and conversations will *say* or *convey something* about what is cultivated in a given group, team, or organization. We thus have to take seriously what the term "value" means, since a value means, *by definition*, something that people regard highly, cherish, or protect. In the case of the self-managing team, we saw that something like solidarity or equity could qualify as a specific value because speaking repeatedly on its behalf means that you are, by definition, attached to or preoccupied with it.

Indeed, if you keep implicitly (or even sometimes explicitly) defending values like solidarity and equity, it means that you are *attached* to them, an attachment that enjoins or leads you to cultivate them in your conversations. What a discursive perspective on organization allows us to unveil is the *performative* character of things like values, norms, and principles, which define what a culture is. Interestingly, this echoes what Van Maanen (2011) says when he notices that:

> Culture simply refers to the meanings and practices produced, sustained, and altered through interaction, and ethnography is the study and representation of culture as used by particular people, in particular places, at particular times. More important perhaps is not what culture is (and the semantic elasticity surrounding the concept), but – and in keeping with pragmatic principles – *what culture does.*" (p. 221; my italics)

As we see in this very nice quote, Van Maanen not only confirms this idea of cultivation (adding the idea of alteration, which marks the evolving character of any culture, given the performative and eventful character of its production for another next first time), but also reminds us that *culture does things.* How can it do something? Precisely, as we will see, through *what* leads people to say what they say or do what they do, that is, the values, principles, and norms that they are attached to, which a discursive perspective can allow us to unveil and unfold.

Rhetorically speaking, we could also notice the activity of *identification*, which is taking place in this interaction, a key notion that has clear links with the questions of (organizational) culture, identity, and, as we will see, ideology (Barker, 1993; Chaput et al., 2011; Cheney, 1983, 1991, 1997, 1999; Tompkins and Cheney, 1985). As Kenneth Burke (1969), the famous rhetorician, noticed in his *Rhetoric of Motives*, identification constitutes a key aspect of our lives, since it is the means by which we can, of course, identify who or what we are, but also persuade or convince others about something because we have the same traits, interests, values, and therefore identity.

Another terminology Burke (1969) is using to convey the idea of identification is *consubstantiality*, a term he borrows from

Christian liturgy and that etymologically means "the fact of having the same substance." Cheney and Tompkins (1987) indeed note that organizational identification implies "the development and maintenance of an individual's or a group's 'sameness' or 'substance' against a backdrop of change and 'outside' elements" (p. 5). The term "substance" thus has to be understood (etymologically, again) as "what stands under" something else (substance comes from the Latin *sub-stare* with *sub* meaning "under" and *stare* meaning "to stand"). Consubstantiality thus refers to the state of sharing what stands under what we are or do.

Although the notions of substance and consubstantiality might sound quite old-fashioned or, even worse, too metaphysical, Burke (1969) reminds us that "substance, in the old philosophies, was an *act*; and a way of life is an *acting-together*; and in acting together, men have common sensations, concepts, images, ideas, attitudes, that make them *consubstantial*" (p. 21; italics in the original; see also Chaput et al., 2011). If *we* are consubstantial, this therefore means that what stands under us (what Burke calls common sensations, concepts, images, ideas, and attitudes) precisely is what identifies us as a group, team, or an organization.

You can identify with someone else because you feel, for instance, that you *share* with him or her some specific sensations, ideas, and attitudes, which define who you are (and therefore who he or she is). Incidentally, this is why identification tends to be closely associated with understanding (under-standing). When you identify with someone else, you want to (or think you can) understand how he or she feels or thinks. Rhetoric thus invites us to analyze organizational discourse and interactions through the way interactants perform and constitute sameness or identification, which is also a way to create, of course, division and separateness from other people.

In our interaction, this tension between identification and division can be felt and analyzed through Martha's and Diego's interventions, but also through Phil's response. One way indeed to interpret what Martha and Diego are telling Phil is to notice that they invite him to ultimately choose if he is *with* or *against* them. How are they doing that? By implicitly reminding him, as pointed out before, what values or principles *matter* or *count* to them as a team (solidarity, equity, as already pointed out). Rhetorically speaking, what Martha and Diego are doing is to *substantiate* the reprimands and reproaches they address to Phil by implicitly reminding him of the values they stand for as a team and the expectations they have.

As they say, it is because Phil does not appear to abide by these values that he is "causing problems." In terms of identification and consubstantiality, we thus see that Martha's and Diego's intervention consists of implicitly *reminding him of the values, principles, and norms which they as a team stand on*, that is, the team's substance, so to speak (remember that the term "substance" should be understood dynamically, not statically), or its identity. Note, incidentally, that what we *stand for* (what we are attached to) is also what stands under us (our substance), given what I have been saying about values and attachment.

It is therefore not surprising to see the tensions, emotions, and even passions that can be felt in this interaction, despite not having access to the video of this specific encounter. As rhetoricians also noticed a long time ago, speech and writing rely not only on language, reasoning, and argumentation (*logos*), combined with the speaker's character, personality, and authority (*ethos*), but also on what animates, moves, or even enthuses him or her, as well as his or her discourse (*pathos*) (Aristotle, 1992). In this discussion, a form of pathos can be felt because what is at least partly at stake is what the participants stand for, which is also what stands under their identity as a team, an identity that Phil is accused of calling into question through his alleged misbehavior.

The *substance* of Martha's and Diego's criticism, that is, what stands under or substantiates it, is also what *leads* them to say what moves them in this discussion. If Phil's alleged misconduct is certainly what triggers this intervention, we could also note that such a misconduct can be identified as such precisely because it deviates or departs from the norms, principles, and values this team is supposed to stand for, defining its identity. The substance of Martha's and Diego's criticism thus points also to what is supposed to be the *substance of their team*, that is, what stands under it, what defines it, what makes it what it is, as reaffirmed for another next first time.

Note also the work that Martha and Diego are doing to reaffirm Phil's identity as a team member – "You're a member of our team" (line 5), "When you work, you do a good job" (lines 12–13), "You're part of the team" (line 22) – which could be understood as a way to remind him how he should identify with or at least respect and stand for what the team stands for. As they define the situation, for him to deviate from this path amounts to forcing them to fire him, as expressed when Martha says, "Don't make us do that" (lines 15–16), even if she never mentions the word "fire" itself.

In terms of how interlocutors define the situation, which is, among other things, what rhetoric invites us to look at, we thus see how Martha puts the onus of responsibility for what is happening on Phil himself. He is the one who ultimately might "make [them] do that" should he decide not to change his behavior, a definition of the situation that Phil appears to acknowledge and de facto accept. As Barker (1999) notes, this kind of control over what is expected from team members is all the more powerful in that it is based on what team members are supposed to have agreed on, *in concert*, the substance or premises of their collective action as a team.

If we now look at this interaction from a **narrative perspective**, we could again notice that no story seems to be explicitly told by Martha, Phil, or Diego. We saw that Martha did accuse Phil of misconduct and warned him that this could have tough consequences for his future in the team, but at no point were we able to identify that she was recounting, say, an anecdote like, for instance, the one Sam Steinberg, was telling in chapter 2. So does it mean that this perspective has nothing to tell us about this specific conversation?

The response is no because what matters is the kind of story or narrative that the participants might be *implicitly* conveying in this conversation. Narrativity is indeed the basic way we *make sense* of the world around us, which implies that any way we interpret a given situation contains, by definition, a narrative component.[2]

Although Martha might not be *explicitly* telling a story or recounting an anecdote to Phil, we have already noticed, for instance, that she is presenting or defining a problematical situation that her intervention is supposed to address and solve.

What is this situation? The fact, as already noticed, that Phil's conduct has been deviating from what is expected from him: "We don't like the pattern you're setting here. You've been late getting back and you're going to get yourself in trouble" (lines 2–3); "This is a bad pattern you have going here" (line 12); "you've started to cause problems. We're worried that we can't depend on you" (lines 20–1). All these turns of talk point to a breach, violation, or infringement, which therefore calls for and justifies her intervention, making her implicit narrative *tellable*. Something eventful deserves to be implicitly recounted and explicitly addressed.

Furthermore, the story that Martha is implicitly depicting appears to display all the features identified by Bruner (1991), including canonicity/breach (5), referentiality (6), and context sensitivity/negotiability (9), that is, three features that were apparently missing in the apartment move illustration in chapter 3. Because there is a breach in the canonical way things are supposed to work in this team (feature 5), sides indeed have to be taken as to what might have triggered or caused it (feature 6), which means that specific perspectives could be negotiated (feature 9).

As we already know, putting forward the existence of a breach indeed presupposes that some canonical script or program has been violated. This shows why narratives (whether implicit or explicit) are especially interesting for the study of identity and culture (and, as we will soon see, ideology). Canonicity indeed implies the existence of norms, rules, and laws ("canon" comes from the Greek *kanōn*, which means "rule" or "measuring stick"), which defines the substance, culture, or identity of a given group or organization.

This explains why some (types of) narratives tend to be *cultivated* in organizations or societies. By being repeated over and over, these narratives contribute to the reproduction of norms, values, standards, principles, rules, or canons that they implicitly or explicitly defend. An organizational culture is thus characterized by the type of stories that people explicitly or implicitly tell, since the telling of these stories says something about the kind of values, norms, or standards that are promoted in a given team or organization. Narratives thus *reaffirm* what, in many respects, define and constitute an organization, that is, its rules, canons, and norms.

Again, Barker (1999) selected this interaction because it was for him representative of the kind of intervention that team members make when something does not seem to work as expected. These interventions can thus be studied from a narrative perspective in identifying the kind of situation that it depicts, a situation that always bears narrative components. For instance, we could note that Martha's intervention can be reconstructed as a story of a (potential) betrayal: inspired by Greimas's (1987) narratology, we could note that Phil is the *mandatee* (the agent, hero, or main character, if you will), but he is a hero who is presented as having to choose whether he wants to remain as such or become a sort of traitor to the cause.

As we also see, Martha implicitly portrays the *mandator* as the team itself in that this latter is identified as the source of expectations regarding what Phil is supposed to do ("You're a member of our team. We *expect* you to support all of us," lines 5–6, my italics). Furthermore, this intervention allows her and Diego to remind Phil of his mandate or mission, which is precisely to "support ... [them]" (lines 6 and 8) in the work they all have to do. As in the case of most narratives, *obstacles* are also introduced when Martha refers to what is causing Phil to deviate from his duties, that is, his relationship with Sandy: "We don't care about your personal life, what you do on your own time. We don't mind you visiting Sandy every now and then. But you've started to cause problems. We're worried we can't depend on you" (lines 18–21). In other words, visiting Sandy now and then is acceptable, but not if it is to the detriment of the job that needs to be done.

As we see, depicting or identifying a situation amounts to implicitly telling a narrative with various protagonists bearing different roles (mandator, mandatee, obstacle, mission). Although this narrative is supposed to *refer* to a given situation (hence, the

105

feature of referentiality, proposed by Bruner, 1991), we also see that such a reference is far from being neutral and transparent. It is, as Taylor and Van Every (2000) remind us, following Greimas (1987), *polemical*. There are bad guys and good guys (Robichaud et al., 2004). In Martha's narrative, the question seems to be "Will Phil remain a good guy, or will he betray the cause and become a bad guy, i.e., someone who deserves to be fired?" This narrative is thus supposed to make a difference in *constituting*, *defining*, or *identifying* a situation that enjoins Phil to choose his side.

A given narrative thus always expresses a viewpoint, preoccupation, or perspective, which can be a priori negotiable (cf. Bruner's (1991) *context sensitivity* and *negotiability*). In this specific case, we see, however, that the negotiation hardly takes place as this poor Phil is prevented from developing his counternarrative. Even if he is the first to speak when he sees his three colleagues coming to him – "I was just coming back. It's not a big deal" (line 1) – his justifications do not seem to work as Martha immediately starts to reprimand him on behalf of the group. In what follows, he is then interrupted twice (lines 4 and 11) and we finally see him acknowledging that he is indeed the source of the problem – "OK, OK" (line 17) – and that he will be more careful in the future – "Yes, I understand, I'll watch myself more. I'm OK" (line 25).

Note how his justification on line 1 amounts to saying that nothing wrong happened: "I was just coming back. It's not a big deal." In other words, since nothing wrong took place, there is, according to him, no event that would be *tellable*, that is, worth telling on his colleagues' part, something, of course, that Martha denies through what she is telling him afterwards. As already noticed, all his subsequent attempts to rehabilitate himself fail as he is interrupted without having a chance to explain or justify his lateness in returning to work.

To that extent, *no negotiation is taking place*, as it is Martha and Diego's narrative – which is also presented as the *team's* narrative – that ultimately prevails. According to them, an event did take place, which triggered a storyline that is not only tellable but also dictates that some action be taken on the team's part, in order to make Phil change his behavior. Although the question of the truth or verisimilitude of this narrative is still relevant, what matters at this point is *how it constitutes or identifies the situation*. Because of the normative dimension of any narrative, this way of telling what is happening is also a way to constitute and identify the norms and values that are important for this team, that is, its identity: helping each other, working hard, being fair with one another, similar to many norms and values we had already identified in our previous analyses.

Unfolding Ideologies from Discourse

Interestingly, this reflection on narratives gives us a nice transition to address the sixth perspective, that is, **critical discourse analysis**, as well as the key question of ideology. In many respects, I, the author of these lines, could be criticized for putting this question at the end of this chapter, as though these aspects just constituted an afterthought on my part. In my defense, my conviction is that I had to first address the questions of culture and identity from the first five perspectives in order to do justice to the question of ideology and the critical approach.

What we have seen so far is how specific speech acts, conversational features, rhetorical moves, semiotic aspects, and narrative mechanisms could contribute to the constitution of a specific organizational culture and identity. In many respects, Fairclough (2005) could point out that what we have done so far is to study discourse as (1) *a text* (in our case, what was *said* by Martha, Phil, and Diego), but also as (2) *a discursive practice* (what Martha, Phil, and Diego did in saying what they said). What would be missing for him would be fully studying discourse as (3) *a social practice*.

Indeed, even if we did study the cultural dimension of Martha's and Diego's discourse, that is, the extent to which discourse contributes to reproducing and constituting specific cultural traits, which reaffirms the identity of their team, what we have not analyzed so far are the *political* and *ideological* dimension of their discourse. In other words, we did not dwell on the extent to which this specific discourse would contribute to reproducing what Fairclough (2005) defines as specific ideological and political structures. According to CDA, not only Phil, but also Martha, Diego, and Marty would be subjected to these structures without necessarily being aware of them.

In order to illustrate this point, I propose that we return to the "theoretical scene" that Althusser (1971) imagined to illustrate how people *get subjected* to a specific ideology or order of discourse. As we remember (cf. chapter 2), this scene portrays a policeman who hails a pedestrian in the street by saying "Hey, you there!," an interpellation that prompts this person to turn round, thus becoming, according to Althusser, a subject. As he notices, the policeman embodies a form of ideology that *constitutes* individuals as subjected to it.

If we compare this scene with the one we just analyzed, some parallels can be easily drawn, but some nuances should be introduced too. For instance, it seems rather obvious, at first sight, that Martha and, to a lesser extent, her colleagues Diego and Marty play the role of Althusser's policeman. Remember how Barker (1999) describes the scene just before the discussion takes place:

> Martha saw that Phil was late, again, getting back to work from a break. She got up from her work on testing, said something to Marty and Diego, two longer-tenured workers on the team, and went to the white team's area. She caught Phil's attention and *beckoned* him to come. She waited for him just behind the red team's area. Marty and Diego joined her. (p. 80; my italics)

The term used by Barker is "beckon," which appears much less strong than hailing, calling out, or interpellating. In comparison with the policeman, Martha thus seems careful not to *publicly* and *openly* hail or signal Phil to come to see her. This absence can be interpreted as an attempt, on her part, to preserve a form of respect vis-à-vis her teammate. Although we know that she intends to reprimand Phil, it does not look as if she wants to humiliate him by chastizing him in front of all his co-workers. Given that self-managing teams are supposed to be *peer* groups, a form of *respect* is also supposed to be cultivated among members. Openly criticizing him in front of everyone could indeed be interpreted as overstepping her right and authority.

Having said that, we can still point out that a form of *subjection* is taking place. First, it is noteworthy, as mentioned before, that it is Phil and not Martha who is speaking first in this scene. As Phil says, "I was just coming back. It's not a big deal" (line 1), a justification that shows how Phil appears to know already that some accusations are about to be formulated. He might be considered *guilty* of something, which is precisely what Althusser (1971) had in mind when he spoke of interpellation. Although Martha, Diego, and Marty have not said anything yet, the fact that Martha beckoned him and is now waiting for him with two longer-tenured workers *speaks for itself*: Phil knows he is in trouble and this is why he starts justifying himself, anticipating the storm that is about to fall on his head.

To some extent, Phil's subjection could thus appear even stronger than in the policeman's case in that *no words even need to be pronounced in order for Phil to start feeling guilty of something*. Semiotically speaking, the gaze and posture of his co-workers waiting for him behind the red team's area seem sufficient to set the scene of his improvised trial. This subjection is then confirmed by what subsequently happens in their conversation. As already noticed, Phil is interrupted twice when he tries to defend himself (lines 4 and 11) and he ends up acknowledging that he made a mistake (lines 17 and 25). For all practical purposes, he thus appears to accept the way Martha and her colleagues define the situation, a situation where he is presented as guilty of misconduct.

If you look back at the analyses we have done in this chapter so far, you can then realize that speech act theory, rhetoric, semiotics, narrative analysis, and conversation analysis can all help us identify this activity of subjection. What CDA adds to this portrait is the fact that this order of discourse – what Alvesson and Kärreman (2000) call big D discourse – functions as "a representation of the imaginary relationship of individuals to their real conditions of existence" (Althusser, 1971: 162). In other words, these beliefs, assumptions, norms, and values that we saw reproduced for another next first time in this discussion are actually hiding the real character of the teammates' conditions of existence and interests.

Interestingly, these are the same conclusions James Barker reached after studying self-management teams in this organization. Concertive control, as he pointed out, is a form of control where workers in *concert with each other* define how things should be done in this kind of team. This form of control is all the more powerful in that it is supposed to come *from the teammates themselves*, making resistance more difficult. As long as orders were coming solely from supervisors, a certain form of solidarity could lead teammates to protect each other from potential retribution on the managers' and supervisors' part. However, with self-management teams, *the "orders" are now coming from the teammates themselves* to the extent that they are supposed to define by themselves how work should be done.

A critical discourse analyst would thus observe that the values of solidarity, equity, justice, respect, or even hard work, which are cultivated and reproduced in this discussion, allow the organization to *delegate control to the workers themselves*. In other words, one way to conceive of a self-management team amounts to saying that it seems a wonderful device to subject teammates to the tyranny of other teammates, a tyranny that is supposed to ultimately serve the organization's interests. In narrative terms, we could also point out that, with such a system, you do not have an opposition between the supervisor (usually portrayed as the bad guy), on the one side, and the supervisees (usually portrayed as the good guys), on the other side. Since everyone is supposed to supervise everyone else, the only bad guy becomes the one who does not comply with what was agreed on by the team members, which is exactly what we see happening in this interaction.

As pointed out in chapter 2, CDA would thus encourage us to analyze what they call the *conditions of possibility* (Foucault, 1989; Fairclough, 2005) of this discussion, that is, what makes it possible, not only in terms of what is said and how it is said (something we have already done so far), but also in terms of *who* is authorized or constrained to say what is said and what author-izes or constrains this person to say what she says. Although team members appear to protect their own interests in supervis-ing and monitoring each other, they also (and especially) protect the company's interests, a protection all the more effective in that it appears to be hidden in comparison with other forms of management.

As long as it was a supervisor who embodied the organization and its interests or preoccupations, teammates had a way to iden-tify the source of their subjection, that is, the organization itself, as well as its interests or preoccupations in terms of profitabil-ity, effectiveness, and viability, as represented by the supervisor. However, when every teammate becomes a potential supervisor, this form of embodiment becomes more *invisible*, since everyone is now speaking and acting in the name of the team and its interests (and not the organization itself, at least directly), as we also saw in the discussion we studied. We are here in the realm of micro-forms of power, that is, regimes of truths that tend to remain more invis-ible because they have been *naturalized* in the way people interact with each other on a daily basis (Deetz, 1992; Foucault, 1977a, 1984).

This confirms what Althusser (1971) noticed when he pointed out that a given ideology is *invisible* to most subjects. This ide-ology, which we could call the self-management ideology, thus recruits subjects by interpellating them, while *denying* its ideologi-cal character. As he wrote, "ideology never says 'I am ideological'" (p. 175). Nobody can indeed be against solidarity, justice, or even hard work, as many principles that we saw are mobilized in the discussion we studied. However, a critical discourse analyst would add that all these noble principles ultimately serve the organiza-tion's interests even if they are never mentioned per se by Martha, Diego, or even Phil.

This kind of analysis thus belongs to what Mumby (1997) calls a *discourse of suspicion*[3] to the extent that critical scholars are usually more interested in what is not said than what is said in a given discussion (see especially Deetz et al., 2007). While the first five perspectives helped us develop what Mumby calls a *discourse of understanding*, critical scholars tend to suspect that what is said and the way it is said actually promote a certain *order of discourse*, which ultimately serve specific interests, in our cases, the owners' and managers' interests.

5

Meetings

Negotiation, Decision-making, and Conflicts

As shown in the previous chapter, discourse can be a site of struggle where many different interests come to be represented and negotiated (Grant et al., 2004; Putnam, 2004). In this chapter, I will show how discursive perspectives can enlighten the phenomena of negotiation, decision-making, and conflicts by focusing on meetings, one of the quintessential activities associated with organizations (Cooren, 2007). As Boden (1994) indeed reminds us:

> Organizations are people. When people come together in organizations to get things done, they talk ... [T]alk, I shall propose, is the lifeblood of all organizations and, as such, it both shapes and is shaped by the structure of the organization itself. Through multiple layers of ordinary talk, people in organizations actually discover, as a deeply and contingent matter, their shared goals, many agendas, environmental uncertainties, potential coalitions, and areas of actual conflict. (p. 8)

Although we already know that organizations should not be reduced to talk (given that an organization gets materialized not only through what its representatives say on its behalf, but also, for instance, through its operations, its buildings, or its shares), Boden (1994) points out that meetings and other conversational episodes that take place in organizations "*constitute* the moments, myths, and through time, the very structuring of the organization" (p. 8; italics in the original). In other words, without conversations and meetings, there would not be any organization (Taylor, 1993; Taylor and Van Every, 2000) even if organizations should not, of course, be *reduced* to talks and texts.

So why are meetings interesting to study from a discursive perspective? Because it is a typical activity where people are supposed to not only exchange their viewpoints, but also to make decisions that can have important bearings on the future of their organization(s). As with any discussions, we will see that a meeting is always situated, located, and circumscribed in a specific time and a specific space (the period during which and the location in which the meeting is taking place), but we will also see that it is intended to participate in and contribute to a larger process that gets *invoked in* and *altered by* what people are talking about.

A meeting (and communication or discourse in general) can thus be considered dislocated or disjointed to the extent that this is where/when the "then" and "there" (whether past or future) get represented and staged in the "here" and "now" (Vasquez, 2013), creating an effect of continuity between the past, present, and future. Although this might sound a little complicated, we will see that these activities of representation and staging constitute the very means by which people get things done (or not done) through talking with each other.

In order to illustrate this point, I propose that we analyze a meeting excerpt that concerns Médecins Sans Frontières (MSF), the famous humanitarian organization (also known as Doctors Without Borders) and winner of the Nobel Peace Prize in 1999. These excerpts are taken from video recordings that I completed during a seven-year research project devoted to the missions that this organization undertakes throughout the world. For this study, the objective was to record and analyze as faithfully as possible the work MSF representatives do on a daily basis to make their humanitarian interventions possible. In order to do that, my assistants, colleagues, and I used the technique of video-shadowing, which consists of following someone while video-recording his or her daily activities (Meunier and Vasquez, 2008; Vasquez, 2013).

The following recording took place in the Democratic Republic of the Congo, more precisely in North Kivu, a region that has been devastated by several wars, which explains the presence of MSF in this part of the world since the 1970s. In these excerpts, Robert, a regional coordinator for MSF, and his subordinate, Marius, a head of mission, are talking with the director of a regional hospital, a hospital that MSF began supporting some six months earlier. Supporting a hospital means that MSF is taking care of the salaries of its employees (which, consequently, increase dramatically) while providing additional equipment and human resources (doctors, administrators, nurses, non-medical staff) to the facilities. MSF also tends to introduce its own medical protocols, which sometimes creates conflicts with hospital directors who feel that their authority is somewhat threatened.

In the excerpt we are about to analyze, Robert, Marius, and the hospital director begin discussing the case of a one-hour meeting that takes place three times a week at the hospital from 8 a.m. until 9 a.m. According to hospital procedures, all members of the medical staff (nurses and physicians) are required to participate in these meetings, which means that none of them is, of course, attending to the patients in their respective wards during this timeframe. Robert and Marius, who speak in the name of MSF, find this situation highly problematic, since the patients are, according to them, being left to themselves, thereby creating a potential health hazard. The hospital director, for his part, thinks that these one-hour meetings should be maintained, since they constitute key updating moments where all staff members are informed of the current situation in the various departments of the hospital.

As sometimes happens in meeting, two positions are thus conflicting with each other, which leads to some negotiation between the two parties. Although this discussion is a little long (it lasts more than 20 minutes), I decided to reproduce it almost entirely, since it gives us an idea of what can typically happen during this kind of conversation where specific courses of action must be decided (after all, meetings do tend to be long, don't they?). As in the previous chapter, we will see what each perspective tells us about the various moves that can be observed during this interaction. However, in contrast with the previous chapters, each excerpt will be analyzed from only one perspective, which will allow us to avoid repetition.

For each perspective, an excerpt of the meeting will be reproduced, followed by a summary of what seems to be happening. I will then show how each specific passage can be analyzed by mobilizing the perspective in question.

Rhetoric

So here is how this excerpt begins:

MSF Excerpt #1

1317	Marius	=Because meanwhile it's the same thing, it's a meeting that lasts
1318		thirty to forty-five minutes, as you were saying last time and we
1319		have no one on the wards any more ((smiling))
1320		(1.0)
1321	Marius	And [at that moment–
1322	Director	[Yes well:: there are always uh mechanisms uh there are
1323		people who always call us and we dispatch a nurse if there is a
1324		problem because these are important update meetings.
1325	Marius	It's not always [like that.
1326	Director	[and uh:
1327	Marius	((repetitively pointing backward with his pen over his shoulder))
1328		There was– Monday there was a problem there and it's uh it's the
1329		expat who was passing by ((repetitively pointing forward with his
1330		pen)) who saw that there was a problem and who had uh to– and
1331		who had to call the nurse otherwise (.) there was nobody who
1332		could see it, the problem.
1333	Director	Yes, no, but it's often the mothers they have uh the instruction (.)
1334		when we are in a meeting if there is a problem (.) of fever, of
1335		convulsion (.) the mother must come inform us.
1336	Marius	Hum.
1337	Director	And then we dispatch a nurse to go over there (.) Well maybe this
1338		mother was absent-minded.

As the excerpt begins, we see Marius, the head of mission, tell his interlocutor, the hospital director, why he thinks this one-hour meeting is problematic. As he points out, no one is on the hospital wards while the meeting takes place (lines 1317–19). This intervention is then followed by a response from the director, who explains why the problem raised by Marius is not really one. As he says, there exist what he calls "mechanisms," which allow them to dispatch someone if there is a problem on the ward (lines 1322–4). Marius then reacts by telling the anecdote of an expat who happened to see that there was a problem and consequently called a nurse (lines 1325–32), which amounts to questioning the reliability of the mechanisms the director is talking about. The director then retorts that the mothers who are at the patients' bedside have instructions to call them if there is a problem (lines 1333–5). If this mother did not call them, it is maybe, according to him, because she "was absent-minded" (line 1338).

Given that we are essentially dealing with argumentative moves here, we will question this first excerpt from a rhetorical perspective. Rhetoric is indeed very well equipped to study controversial situations as well as conflicts, in that it consists of analyzing how people manage to find "in any particular case all the available means of persuasion" (Aristotle). As mentioned in the second chapter, rhetoric is first and foremost concerned with the *power of words*, that is, their capacity to make a difference in a specific context. How do Marius and the director try to make a difference through their respective interventions here? By defining, each in their own way, *a situation*.

As the famous rhetorician Lloyd F. Bitzer (1968) noticed almost 50 years ago, rhetoric is indeed *situational* because "rhetorical discourse comes into existence as a response to a situation, in the same sense that an answer comes into existence in response to a question, or a solution in response to a problem" (p. 5). As he also points out, "One might say metaphorically that every situation *prescribes* its fitting responses: the rhetor may or may not read the prescription accurately" (p. 11; my italics). Something Bitzer did not dwell on, however, is that situations are not always that clear about their identity and about what they tell, dictate, or prescribe to us. For instance, we see here how the two interlocutors basically disagree about what the situation facing them calls for or demands.

If we look in detail at how they argue for their respective positions, we indeed note that Marius and the director keep *presenting facts* to each other, a series of facts that are supposed to portray a specific case, situation, or reality. Marius introduces a first fact, which he presents as being corroborated by the director himself: "it's a meeting that lasts thirty to forty-five minutes, *as you were saying last time*" (lines 1317–18). By mentioning that it is the director himself who actually said that the meeting lasted 30 to 45 minutes, Marius thus tries to reinforce the objective character of the situation he is presenting. It is not only he, Marius, who is saying that the meeting lasts 30 to 45 minutes, but the director too, which is intended to increase the impartiality or objectivity of this claim. Rhetorically speaking, we thus see a move on Marius's part to establish the truth of his affirmation by invoking what his interlocutor might have said.

He then goes on with the presentation of another fact that is portrayed as the consequence of the first: "and we have no one on the wards any more" (lines 1318–19). Interestingly, this fact is presented as *speaking for itself*, since we do not hear Marius drawing any specific conclusion from the claim he just made. Why is this fact supposed to speak for itself? Because it is supposed to tell the director (and whoever is made aware of it) that there is indeed a problem. Rhetorically speaking, this move on Marius's part thus consists of *establishing the obviousness of his position*. Presenting facts that are supposed to speak for themselves implies that the way Marius depicts the situation is not controversial and should be clear in terms of its reading and interpretation. "And we have no one on the wards any more" *speaks for itself* because everyone is supposed to know and understand that there should be at least one staff member present on the hospital wards at any time.

In response, the director comes up, however, with his own version of the situation, a situation where mechanisms exist to anticipate any problems that might occur while the meeting is taking place ("Yes well:: there are always uh mechanisms uh there are people who always call us and we dispatch a nurse if there is a problem because these are important update meetings," lines

1322–4). In other words, the aspect of the situation that the director is presenting is supposed to reassure Marius. While the latter
just raised concerns about meetings he portrays as problematical,
the director responds by highlighting the existence of procedures
that are supposed to appease these concerns. Furthermore, he also
highlights that the meetings Marius is calling into question are
"important update meetings," which amounts to establishing their
legitimacy. Given that they are important, their existence should
not be questioned.

As we see, rhetoric is *situational* because the situations that these
two interlocutors depict, portray, or present are supposed to *raise
concerns* or, on the contrary, *appease them*. As we already saw
in chapter 4, rhetoric indeed refuses to detach *logos* (the words
pronounced during this discussion) from *pathos* (what is supposed
to animate this discussion) and *ethos* (the interlocutors' character, personality, and authority). What does this mean concretely?
That both Marius and the director are trying to establish their
own authority through the authority of their respective positions
(*ethos*), but that doing this consists of showing what animates,
concerns, or moves them (*pathos*).

Raising concerns or preoccupations (which is what Marius is
doing here) indeed amounts to staging or presenting aspects of the
context that are supposed to preoccupy, worry, or concern anyone
who would be made aware of them. In other words, it is as though
Marius were saying: here are matters of concern, that is, things
that not only preoccupy me (*pathos*), but also legitimize my position (*ethos*) according to which some intervention is in order; my
concerns should therefore be yours too, since they are legitimate.

While Marius insists on aspects of the situation that should
ignite or trigger an intervention on their part – "there is no one
on the wards any more," "Monday there was a problem" – we
see the director insisting on aspects of the situation that are meant
to extinguish the ignition or deactivate the trigger, so to speak.
Although the transcription by itself does not allow us to illustrate
this aspect, it is noteworthy that Marius looks concerned when
he makes his point, while the director appears quite calm and
serene. In other words, pathos can be felt not only through what

is said, but also through the two protagonists' bodies, postures, and gestures.

Furthermore, we notice that at no point do Marius and the director explicitly say that they disagree with each other. What we see is that they present different facts that are supposed to show, demonstrate, or prove that there is or is not a problem. Everything thus happens as if it were not only *they* – Marius and the director – who were saying that there was or was not a problem, but also the *situations* they are depicting each in their own way. In terms of authority (or ethos), mobilizing aspects of a situation thus consists of *lending weight* to their respective positions.

While we just saw that the director mobilizes the customs and procedures of the hospital in order to appease Marius's concerns ("there are *always* uh mechanisms uh there are people who *always* call us and we dispatch a nurse if there is a problem"), Marius responds by invoking an anecdote that implies that these procedures are, in fact, not as safe as implied by the director ("There was– Monday there was a problem there and it's uh it's the expat who was passing by ((repetitively pointing forward with his pen)) who saw that there was a problem and who had uh to – and who had to call the nurse otherwise (.) there was nobody who could see it, the problem," lines 1328–32).

While the customs and procedures presented by the director are aimed at legitimizing the fact that these meetings take place, this anecdote amounts to questioning this legitimacy. *Arguing for or against a specific position thus consists of staging various aspects of a situation that corroborate this position or not.* Arguments are therefore made of aspects of a situation that people want to put forward in a discussion. While the procedures and customs of the hospital are supposed to *tell us* that everything is fine with these meetings (the director's position), the expat and his anecdote are supposed to *tell us* that these meetings are questionable (Marius's position).

Rhetoric thus invites us to realize that *facts and values cannot be dissociated from each other*, that is, that there is no such thing as a value-free fact (a similar position can be found in John Dewey (1916) and Charles Sanders Peirce (1877), who were not rhetoricians, but pragmatist philosophers). Each fact respectively presented by Marius and the director is indeed supposed to tell us *what should be done* or *what should not be done* about the meetings, hence the idea that some actions are valued while others are not. For instance, when the director responds, "Yes, no, but it's often the mothers they have uh the instruction (.) when we are in a meeting if there is a problem (.) of fever, of convulsion (.) the mother must come inform us. And then we dispatch a nurse to go over there (.) Well maybe this mother was absent-minded" (lines 1333–8), he is presenting another fact that is supposed to tell Marius that there is already a mechanism in place (he speaks here in terms of instructions) and that if there is something or someone to be blamed, it should be the mother who was absent-minded, not the meetings themselves.

All in all, while the facts presented by Marius are supposed to value or promote change, the ones presented by the director value or promote a form of status quo. Each fact presented by a party thus consists of settling a situation that either calls for change (Marius) or, on the contrary, calls for the reproduction of the same (the director). In terms of constitution, we thus see that the meeting is constituted by these rhetorical moves that consist of *making a situation speak*. The meeting is therefore not detached from its context. It is, on the contrary, the way by which what matters to the participants will express itself and be addressed. So let us now see what semiotics can reveal about a subsequent excerpt.

Semiotics

Here is how the discussion evolves a few minutes later:

MSF Excerpt #2

1407	Robert	Wouldn't it be more construct– Wouldn't you have more
1408		constructive discussions with a smaller group (.) Uh, personally I
1409		understand, I understand very well the idea of having updates,
1410		transmissions, etcetera ((turning his head toward Marius)), it's:::
1411	Marius	Hum, [certainly

1412	Robert	[Marius, he says these– these meetings are very good (.) It's
1413		just that it's a lot of people (.) and that it leaves (.) nobody on the
1414		wards uh during an important hour of the day from 8:00 a.m. to
1415		9:00 a.m.↑ (.) uh:: wouldn't it be more constructive to do that
1416		with the department heads (.) with the physicians (.) uh: and
1417		following this it is the department heads who relay in their wards
1418		(.) with their teams. I don't know uh, it's–
1419	Director	Yes, this uh this is heavy uh because even the transmission of the
1420		message (.) uh changes from one level to another↑ (.) Each person
1421		relays the way he understood (1.0) and uh <u>we</u> wish to always stay
1422		with everybody and each and everyone understands uh he draws
1423		uh from the source (1.0) he is [not
1424	Robert	[It means it means one hour– it
1425		means three hours per week where there is no one in the– in the
1426		hospital ((looking at the director with a light smile))
1427	Director	Yes uh and then the risks that are:: already– because we have to
1428		start from the risks that we have already run during (.) these few
1429		minutes.
1430	Marius	Well
1431	Director	I think that::: the ideal situation is uh to give the opportunity to
1432		everyone (.) to:: be able uh to participate in these meetings (.)
1433		and:: to have uh:: uh a – a level that is updated everyday.
1434	Robert	But[::
1435	Director	[Becau[se uh
1436	Marius	[Yes but there–
1437	Robert	[Yes but after there is the doctor's visit through– in
1438		each ward [during which he can=
1439	Marius	[Yes (.) that's it
1440	Robert	=During which there should be uh:: this idea of transmission or
1441		updating uh:: too↑
1442	Director	Often time it's not easy because uh:: this meeting, it's a meeting
1443		where uh all the nurses from all the services meet with each other
1444		(.) and the department head or the head of pediatrics he has his
1445		nurses over there=
1446	Robert	=Uhuh↑=
1447	Director	=If there is a pediatric case uh if someone asks him a question, he
1448		can explain (.) if he wants to explain, he explains (.) if he does not
1449		want, well he does uh his rounds, the visit of the patients and then
1450		he passes
1451		(1.0)

1452	Director	And the one who is now in surgery, how will he know what is
1453		happening in internal medicine (.) because <u>we</u> always want to
1454		have nurses who are versatile (.) and who can serve uh at any
1455		moment in other services (.) in case of emergency=

So what is happening in this excerpt of the meeting? First, we see Marius's boss, Robert, trying to reconcile two positions (Marius's and the director's) that appear so far incompatible. How does Robert do this? By proposing to organize meetings that would gather fewer people (line 1407–8) while recognizing the importance of these meetings (lines 1409–10), a recognition that Marius even echoes on line 1411. Robert then takes the opportunity of Marius's alignment to add that Marius actually values these meetings (line 1412), a move that can be understood as an attempt to establish a rapprochement between Marius and the director. Echoing what Marius said previously, Robert then reiterates that there seem to be too many people in these meetings, leaving "nobody on the wards uh during an important hour of the day from 8:00 a.m. to 9:00 a.m." (lines 1413–15).

Having reaffirmed the problematic character of the meetings, Robert then puts forward a detail of his solution: requiring only the physicians and department heads to attend these meetings would allow the latter to relay what is discussed to their own teams on the wards (lines 1415–18). The director reacts to this proposition by mentioning the unpractical character of Robert's solution ("Yes, this uh this is heavy," line 1419), arguing that the presence of intermediaries would increase the risk of discrepancy in the way the information is relayed (lines 1420–3). For the director, the meetings should thus remain as they are, since everyone who participates can then "draw uh from the source" (lines 1422–3).

Robert then interrupts the director by reaffirming (and specifying) what these meetings still mean in terms of absence on the hospital wards ("It means it means one hour– it means three hours per week where there is no one in the– in the hospital," lines 1424–6) while looking at the director with a light smile as if to express the obvious character of the problem. The director then responds by invoking the (absence of) risk associated with this non-attendance. As he points out, what ought to be the basis of their reflection are the risks they have run in the past during what he presents as the "few minutes" (lines 1428–9) during which these meetings take place. While Robert insists on the number of *hours* these meetings represent (three hours per week), the director thus responds by speaking in terms of *minutes*, as if to minimize the level of risk.

While Marius tries to intervene, the director goes ahead by reaffirming what the ideal situation is, that is, "give the opportunity to everyone (.) to:: be able uh to participate in these meetings (.) and:: to have uh:: uh a – a level that is updated everyday" (lines 1431–3). We then see Robert making a new attempt to demonstrate the value of his solution by telling the director that the physicians who will have participated in these meetings will be able to assure the transmission and updating of information to their staff (lines 1437–41). However, the director again responds by reaffirming the inclusive character of the meetings (lines 1442–5) while implying that Robert's solution would actually depend on the physicians' goodwill. In other words, some physicians might not want to diffuse the information to their staff (lines 1447–50). Furthermore, Robert's solution would not allow staff from a specific ward to know what is happening in another ward, while staff members are supposed to be versatile and must be able to "serve uh at any moment in other services (.) in case of emergency" (lines 1454–5).

Having described what happened in this excerpt, I now propose that we analyze it from a semiotic perspective. As you remember, *semiotics* insists that the world people experience is not only meaningful, but that it also actively *tells them* things that they interpret. What we see taking place in this excerpt (and in the previous one too) is that Robert and Marius, on one side, and the director, on the other side, are not only confronting their respective interpretations of the situation, but also telling their interlocutor what this situation literally requires, dictates, or demands, an analysis that appears to echo the idea of rhetorical situation (Bitzer, 1968) that we mobilized previously.

Semiotics adds to rhetoric, however, in that it allows us to reveal *all the elements* that end up participating in the confrontation of these two opposite viewpoints. A situation is not only made of facts that people present to each other as matters of concern (something that rhetoric, as we just saw, shows very well), but of principles, values, rules, traditions, types, habits, and so on, that they implicitly or explicitly mobilize in their discussion and that also matter to them. In other words, semiotics helps us recognize that facts – as any signs – *have to be made to say things* and that in order for them to say things, a sort of *law, principle, value, type,* or *rule* has to be – at least implicitly – mobilized (see Lorino, 2014; Robichaud, 2006; Taylor and Van Every, 2011).

As discussed in chapter 2, a runny nose, a sore throat, and a cough can tell a physician that a person is suffering from a bad cold because the physician *knows* that there is a physical connection between the disease and these symptoms. In other words, she knows that this disease expresses itself through these symptoms/facts, which allows her to read, interpret, and make sense of them. It is this causal connection, which she knows and learned, that, *ceteris paribus,* leads or authorizes her to diagnose that the patient suffers from a bad cold. As mentioned in chapter 2, this connection is what semioticians call the interpretants, which always take the form of habits, laws, principles, values, types, or rules.

In this case, the fact that a disease called a "bad cold" causes a runny nose, a sore throat, and a cough is the sort of law or principle that not only governs her interpretation/diagnostic, but also her recommendations. Although "bad cold causes a runny nose, a sore throat, and a cough" is a fact, it is a fact that is considered to be established or proven. In other words, it has been institutionalized, hence its status of law or principle. It is a source of *authority* (Cooren, 2010; Taylor and Van Every, 2011). It is this institutional fact that leads or authorizes the physician to read or interpret these other facts or tokens that she observes. This is what leads or authorizes her to say what she says.

For the world to say something, people have to be able to read it, which is what semiotics allows us to explain through the notion of interpretant. To read is to re-establish connections that have been learned and already established. Even if the discussion that takes place between Marius, Robert, and the director appears to greatly differ from the physician illustration I just used, we will see that the contrast actually comes from the *disagreement* that opposes Marius and Robert, on one side, and the director, on the other side.

Imagine, for instance, that someone would question the physician about what leads and authorizes her to make her diagnosis. She could then respond, "What makes me think it is a bad cold is that it is a well-established fact that bad colds *typically* have these kinds of symptoms." In her response, we thus see her staging *what* authorizes and leads her to say what she says, the *what* in question being not only the tokens, that is, the symptoms or facts she is observing, but also the type, principle, or law she is mobilizing to make her diagnosis. This is what allows her to read the situation in a specific way. She is therefore staging the interpretant that allows her to make the connection between the representamens (the symptoms) and their object (the disease).

As we will now see, the same phenomenon actually takes place in the second excerpt I reproduced above. Robert, Marius, and the director indeed keep staging or presenting what leads or authorizes them to say what they say, which is a way to legitimize or lend weight to their respective positions. From lines 1407 to 1408, we thus see Robert proposing a solution ("Wouldn't it be more construct– Wouldn't you have more constructive discussions with a smaller group,"), which is then followed by his presentation of principles or values to which he and indirectly Marius declare their attachment ("Uh, personally I understand, I understand very well the idea of having updates, transmissions, etcetera ((turning his head toward Marius)), it's::... Marius, he says these– these meetings are very good," lines 1408–12).

The meetings they are talking about are very good *because* they offer opportunities for updates and transmission, which is something that is implicitly presented as *valued* by Robert and Marius. Robert then points out that the way these gatherings are presently organized is, however, problematic: "It's just that it's a lot of people (.) and that it leaves (.) nobody is on the wards uh during an important hour of the day from 8:00 a.m. to 9:00 a.m." (lines

1412–15). As we see, Robert is not only presenting a fact, situation, or token that is supposed to speak for itself (the absence of personnel in the wards during an important hour of the day), but if this fact, situation, or token manages to speak, it is also because a principle is implicitly mobilized.

What is this principle? A principle of *safety* according to which there should always be personnel on the hospital ward at any time in case something happens to the patients. It is a principle that is never made explicit in the discussion because it should be taken for granted by the interlocutors. It is therefore *in the name of* this principle that Robert suggests holding discussions with a smaller group, that is, this principle of safety requires, according to him, that the meetings take place with a smaller group, which he later describes as composed of department heads and physicians (lines 1415–16), who would then relay the information to their respective team on the ward (lines 1417–18).

Two principles (or interpretants) are therefore implicitly called upon by Robert. On the one hand, *a principle of transmission of knowledge* according to which it is a good thing to keep the hospital personnel updated and, on the other hand, a *principle of safety* according to which patients should not be left by themselves on the wards. While the first principle – transmission – requires, according to Robert, that meetings take place regularly, the second principle – safety – dictates that these meetings be organized with smaller groups. As we see, the situation that Robert mobilizes is not only made of facts, but also of values and principles, which are implicitly convoked in the discussion. *Without these principles and values, the situation could not say anything.*

Interestingly, we then see the director replying to Robert by invoking another principle, according to which transmission should be direct and not mediated by intermediaries. As he says, "Yes, this uh this is heavy uh because even the transmission of the message (.) uh changes from one level to another↑ (.) Each person relays the way he understood (1.0) and uh we wish to always stay with everybody and each and everyone understands uh he draws uh from the source" (lines 1419–23). The director thus devalues and questions Robert's proposal in the name of a principle of direct transmission to which he declares his implicit attachment. In other words, this principle dictates that the meetings take place with everyone in the hospital so that each person can draw the information from the source.

Robert then interrupts the director by reaffirming what it would mean to keep these meetings as they are: "It means it means one hour– it means three hours per week where there is no one in the– in the hospital ((looking at the director with a light smile))" (lines 1424–6). Interestingly, Robert's reaction gives us access to his own *semiosis*, that is, to how signs function or operate for him (see chapter 2): these meetings (*representamen*) stand for (or mean) three hours per week with no one in the hospital (*object*) because of the causal connection that has been established between these two facts (*interpretant*).

But the semiosis does not end here, as Robert and Marius have, from the beginning of the discussion, presented the object itself as problematic. In other words, the object also is itself a representamen: three hours per week with no one in the hospital (*representamen*) stands for (or means) safety hazard for the patients (*object*) because of the causal connection that is, according to Robert (and Marius), generally established between the two (*interpretant*).

As we see, the world that surrounds Robert, Marius, and the director speaks to them (and to us) through semiosis. While holding a meeting with a smaller group would be, for the director, the sign of – that is, it would mean or stand for – an impoverished form of transmission, it would be the sign of a safer environment for the patients. In contrast, holding a meeting with all the hospital staff is, for Robert, the sign of an unsafe environment for the patients, while it is the sign of a good transmission and updating of knowledge to the hospital staff. The fact that X is the sign of Y for someone means that X *says or tells* Y to that person. As the sore throat says or tells something to the physician, the holding of these meetings says or tells two different things to Robert and the director.

This discussion, and all meetings you will observe, thus consists of convoking or staging a series of facts or tokens – for example,

the way the present meetings are organized, the absence of personnel on the hospital wards – that are implicitly presented as signs of
something problematic or not problematic depending on the principles, values, or types that are also implicitly convoked or staged,
such as the fact that hospitals should be safe environments for
patients or the fact that hospital staff should be directly informed
from the source. These elements end up requiring or dictating that
specific actions be taken or not (changing the way these meetings
are organized or keeping them as they are).

All the richness of a discussion comes from the variety of elements that will be convoked by the participants. For instance,
we then see the director replying, "Yes uh and then the risks that
are:: already– because we have to start from the risks that we have
already run during (.) these few minutes" (lines 1427–9). Starting
from the risks that they have already run while these meetings
were taking place, as the director now proposes to do, is a way
to not only minimize the problem (he is not speaking of hours,
as Robert is doing, but of minutes), but also to convoke the past
and the risks that these meetings might have run before. Although
he does not say it explicitly, chances are, according to him, that
examining the level of risk from the past would tell them – that is,
would *give the sign or signal* – that there is no problem with these
meetings. In other words, the past would tell them that these meetings are, in fact, safe.

Having mobilized the past and what it would say, the director can then reaffirm that "the ideal situation is uh to give the
opportunity to everyone (.) to:: be able uh to participate in these
meetings (.) and:: to have uh:: uh a – a level that is updated
everyday" (lines 1431–3). This ideal situation is, we understand,
the present situation, which dictates that nothing be changed or
altered. As we see, he proposes to read/interpret the situation from
a principle to which he implicitly claims his attachment. This is
what appears to *matter* or *count* to him. This is what thus appears
to lead him to say what he says.

Robert then tries once again to show why the solution they
propose would allow the director to meet his concerns for transmission ("Yes but after there is the doctor's visit through– on each

ward during which he can ... During which there should be uh::
this idea of transmission or updating uh:: too↑" (lines 1437–41).
In other words, you think that meetings with a smaller group
mean or stand for bad transmission, while we, Marius and I,
believe that transmission and updating can fully take place afterwards, when the doctor visits the ward. As he did previously, the
director turns this latest attempt down flat, invoking, this time, the
necessity to allow nurses to meet with each other (a possibility that
the meetings presently offer), as well as the doctors' willingness to
share information, which is something that the director does not
control.

As we realize throughout this analysis, semiotics helps us show
how the participants in this meeting constantly mobilize, stage, and
invoke ideal and factual elements that are implicitly or explicitly
presented as saying, meaning, or dictating that something should
be changed or not. In terms of constitution, we observe that any
meeting is therefore the opportunity to redefine *what matters* or
what counts, that is, what should be *signaled*, in a given situation.
These signs or signals are important, since they are supposed to tell
people what should be done. If they are not convoked or evoked,
they will not make a difference in the discussion, that is, they will
not matter, even if they could or should have.

But let us see now what speech act theory can tell us about what
happens just after.

Speech Act Theory

Here is how the discussion evolves.

MSF Excerpt #3

1456	Marius	Yeah but in that case too, we could– we can– we could also think
1457		of a rotation of nurses in each service every other month?
1458		(1.0)
1459	Director	Well (.) these are uh:: propositions that we cannot::: say yes now
1460		(.) This needs to be further pursued uh so uh we always have to
1461		start with numbers (.) as you often say (.) so we say that during a
1462		period in such and such service there were how many prob-

1463		problems while we were at the meeting (.) If we note [that::
1464	Robert	[If we are
1465		not there we cannot know ((with a light smile))
1466	Director	Yes uh we will [know
1467	Robert	[hu hu hu ((laughters))
1468	Director	hu hu [hu
1469	Robert	[hu hu
1470	Director	We will know because during the rounds the mother will explain
1471		uh will say "Well (.) my kid had a crisis at that time"=
1472	Robert	=It's not always easy when we have a doctor in front of us, with a
1473		nurse to tell them uh:: to complain ((looking intently at the
1474		director with a light smile))
1475		(0.5)
1476	Director	Yes (.) that's what they [do::
1477	Robert	[People won't complain of that hu=
1478	Director	=That they do often. Personally I remember when (.) I visited the
1479		patients in pediatrics uh it was the mothers who were inform—
1480		who were informing me that well (.) for instance uh such or such
1481		nurse did not check the vital signs↑ (.) and automatically I was
1482		calling out the nurse (.) so it is the mothers who uh give us the
1483		information (.) and:: personally I think that:: this is not really:: a
1484		problem (.) that is presently alarming↑=

As we see, Marius makes a new attempt by proposing another solution: the possibility to rotate nurses between services (lines 1456–7). This time, the director does not call this latest proposition into question and prefers to avoid it, alleging that all the propositions made so far cannot be decided during the current meeting (lines 1459–60). To justify his position, we see him invoking again the necessity to examine in depth the situation by measuring the number of incidents that might have occurred during past meetings. Robert then interrupts him by arguing that they will not be able to know these numbers, since nobody remains in the wards to notice these incidents (line 1463–4).

Robert's position is then countered by the director who, on the contrary, claims that they will be able to know because the patients' mothers (most of the patients in the hospital are children) do not hesitate to speak up and tell the staff when an incident occurs (lines 1470–1). Robert then retorts that it is not always easy to complain to a doctor with a nurse, implying that the status difference between the mother and the physician can render this type of action difficult (lines 1472–3). Invoking his past experience as a physician, the director then replies that mothers, on the contrary, do not hesitate to speak up (lines 1476–84).

So far, we focused, with rhetoric and semiotics, on how the participants were confronting their respective definitions of the situation, a situation made not only of facts that are presented, but also of ideals and principles that appear to lead them to propose alternative courses of action. With speech act theory, I now propose to focus on what is, more broadly, *accomplished* during these meetings, but also on *who* or even *what* is *doing something* or is *active* in this specific situation. A constitutive view of communication indeed implies that we pay attention not only to the way people co-construct and co-define a situation (even if, as we saw so far, there is not much co-construction and co-definition on the participants' part; it is more a confrontation of definitions!), but also on what or who can make a difference and how differences can be made through communication.

Speech act theory, as we know, reminds us that doing things with words implies that the acts be performed in the *right circumstances*, by the *right person* with the *right words*. As mentioned in chapter 2, this approach thus invites us to pay attention to the question of *authority*, a key topic in organizational studies (Cooren, 2010; Taylor and Van Every, 2011). In the previous chapters, we dealt with situations where authority was somehow not called into question because it was generally acknowledged by the participants. Clearly, this is not what is happening in the meeting we analyze here, since the two parties present keep questioning each other's positions and propositions. The game, if you will, thus consists, for each party, of showing what *authorizes* or *does not authorize* them to say what they say.

We already saw, in chapter 3, that the notions of *author* and *authority* have a common Latin root, *auctor*, which means father, creator, or genitor, the one who initiates, protects, and sanctions. But Benveniste (1969) also reminds us that *auctor* itself comes from the Latin word *augere*, which means to augment, increase, or expand. Being in authority or establishing one's authority thus consists of augmenting, increasing, or expanding the number of authors who/that are accomplishing a given action (Benoit-Barné and Cooren, 2009).

For instance, a jury foreman who declares, in a court of law and after deliberations, "We, the jury, find the defendant to be guilty of the charge of first-degree murder," is not only the right person following the right procedure in the right circumstances. *She is also mobilizing a series of authors who augment the performativity of what is happening* (Cooren and Matte, 2010). When she is speaking, it is indeed not only (1) *she* who is indeed declaring that the defendant is guilty, but also and maybe especially (2) *all the jurors* that she is implicitly referring to when she says "We"; (3) the *jury* itself as a legal body, which is also referred to in her declaration; (4) the tribunal, that this jury represents at this moment of the procedure; (5) the *common public*, which the jury is supposed to represent during the whole process; and even by extension (6) *society* itself, which is ultimately represented in this decision. The person who is declared guilty of first-degree murder is not only declared to be so by the jury foreman, but also by all these entities that implicitly or explicitly participate in the accomplishment of this act.

As soon as there is a relation of authority, there is a relation of *authorship* (Taylor and Van Every, 2011), which means that *the number of authors augments*. The authors of this declaration include the jury foreman, who speaks in the name of the jurors, who made a collective decision on behalf of the jury, which is acting, at this point, for the tribunal, but also for the common public and for society itself. As soon as you have expressions such as "in the name of," "on behalf of," "for," "as the proxy of," "in the stead of," but also, as we will see, "in the best interests of," "for the sake of," "for the good of," "in consideration of," or "out of concern for," you know that the number of authors is assumed to increase and that the authority of what is said might also be augmented.

In our meeting, however, the situation is a little different. We, of course, also have effects of delegation, representation, and authority. When Robert and Marius are speaking, it is also MSF that is deemed to be saying something. While there is no reference to MSF per se in the excerpts we are analyzing, the director invited Robert and Marius to his office as representatives of this organization, which is sponsoring his hospital. Similarly, when the director is speaking, it is also the hospital that is talking, or at least an important and central voice of this institution.

Beyond these obvious effects of representation, delegation, and authority, we will now see that other *voices* can be heard and unfolded in this excerpt, precisely because the three protagonists are trying to find alternative sources of authority/authorship in order to put forward their respective positions. In other words, we will observe how Marius, Robert, and the director are implicitly trying to *augment* the number of authors of what is put forward, hoping that a bigger difference can be made and that their interlocutor might therefore be convinced by what they say. As we will see, this is essentially happening because they present themselves as speaking *out of concern for, for the good of*, or *in consideration of* specific matters that are deemed to be expressing themselves in this situation.

So how does this happen? Let us look at the beginning of the third excerpt. On lines 1456–7, we see Marius propose a new solution that could help them find a meeting point with the director ("Yeah but in that case too, we could – we can – we could also think of a rotation of nurses in each service every other month?"). Although he is the one who proposes something, we also see that the proposition amounts to staging a "we" that implicitly includes the director. This proposition invites the director to think *with* Marius and Robert about the possibility of rotating nurses every other month. The presence of the pronoun "we" in this speech act thus tends to re-create or even perform a unity that has, so far, being completely absent.

After a one-second silence, which often marks the prelude to what will eventually be the rejection of an invitation (Heritage, 1984), the director dodges the proposition by invoking the impossibility to make decisions at this point ("Well (.) these are uh:: propositions that we cannot::: say yes now," lines 1459). This claim, which is presented as a fact, is immediately followed by what, to some extent, *authorizes* or *allows* him to make it ("This needs to be further pursued uh so uh we always have to start with numbers (.) as you often say (.)," lines 1460–1). In terms of authority, the director thus implicitly invokes the need to further pursue the examination of the propositions that have been made so far.

It is therefore *out of concern for* the validity of these propositions that he proposes to postpone the decision. Figuratively speaking, it is therefore this principle – validity – that is supposedly express-ing itself at this point. What does this principle say, according to the director? It *dictates* (another speech act) precisely that they suspend making the decision. It is therefore what he makes this principle say in these circumstances, lending weight and authority to his own position. Although this invocation could, at first sight, look artificial (in other words, it could appear to be "made up" for the circumstances), we see that the director does not hesitate to specify, "as you often say," which is a way to remind his interlocu-tors that *this concern is supposed to be theirs as well.*

In other words, everything happens as if the director was in agreement with Marius and Robert: "You often say that we have to start with numbers in order to validate what we propose to do, I am basically telling you the same thing. What I am saying is essen-tially what you could have said." The weight of this principle thus seems all the more important now that it is presented as a principle that also animates the two MSF representatives. To his own voice, and the voice of this principle, it is therefore as if the director was adding MSF's voice. All of them are presented as dictating that the decision be postponed.

Having established this multiple authorship, he can immediately add, "so we say that during a period in such and such service there were how many prob- problems while we were at the meeting (.) If we note that::" (lines 1461–3). To the inclusive "we" mobilized by Marius in the previous turn, the director thus replies with his own version of this pronoun, a "we" that also includes Robert and Marius and is presented as saying what ought to be done to ascer-tain the number of incidents and validate the propositions made so far. While Marius's previous intervention consisted of proposing something that they all could do, the director responds by directly talking in the name of the three participants.

As we see so far, the speech acts produced in this meeting are often presented as performed not only by the person who voices them, but also by the people who are round the table. It is a way for each participant to create the conditions of a unity, even if this unity can, at any moment, be called into question.

This is actually what happens immediately after, when Robert reacts to what the director has just said, alleging that, "If we are not there we cannot know ((with a light smile))" (lines 1464–5). In other words, nobody will be able to collect the number of incidents, since everybody is supposed to be present at the meetings. This claim, which is presented as a fact, thus amounts to questioning what the director has just proposed, showing that it is not feasible. Although Robert's light smile could mean many things, it could be interpreted as a way to mark the somewhat comical or even absurd character of the situation.

Robert's move also looks like the director's to the extent that both contributions consist of showing that what the other party proposes *cannot* be done. While we saw that the director invoked the necessity to evaluate (almost scientifically) the validity of MSF's propositions before implementing them, Robert invokes, on his side, the infeasibility of what the director has just proposed. As we already know, any speech act is supposed to be produced *in the right circumstances by the right person with the right words*. One of the means that people have at their disposal to counter what their interlocutor is saying thus consists of showing that the latter is *unable* or *unauthorized* to do what s/he is doing, that is, *that the circumstances are not the right ones*. If you look at what is happening from the beginning of their conversation, you realize that this is what is ultimately happening.

But the director does not give up, and retorts, "Yes uh we will know" (line 1466), a counterclaim that he immediately backs up with what, according to him, authorizes him to say what he says: "We will know because during the rounds the mother will explain uh will say 'Well (.) my kid had a crisis at that time'" (lines 1470–

1). The discussion thus now revolves around a battle of predictions about what they will be able to know. And as for any prediction, the key question is again what allows the person to make it (are the circumstances the right ones?). In this case, we see that the director does not hesitate to stage what a mother will, according to him, say, going as far as reproducing her voice in the conversation. Everything thus happens as if the director wanted to counter the questionable character of his prediction by the concrete character of a situation where a mother is staged as speaking up.

Almost unsurprisingly, Robert then questions the director's prediction, invoking the difference of status that exists between a mother and a doctor: "It's not always easy when we have a doctor in front of us, with a nurse to tell them uh:: to complain ((looking intently at the director with a light smile))" (lines 1472–4). This difference, according to him, might prevent the mother from speaking up, which contradicts the director's claim. Again, we see how Robert's reply consists of showing that the circumstances are not the ones his interlocutor presumes they are, that is, they do not authorize the director to make the prediction he is making about the mothers' conduct.

The director then reiterates his claim, invoking this time his past experience as a physician: "That they do often. Personally I remember when (.) I visited the patients in pediatrics uh it was the mothers who were inform- who were informing me that well (.) for instance uh such or such nurse did not check the vital signs↑ (.) and automatically I was calling out the nurse (.) so it is the mothers who uh give us the information (.) and:: personally I think that:: this is not really:: a problem (.) that is presently alarming↑" (lines 1478–84). What does this past experience say, according to him? That mothers do not hesitate to speak up, which ultimately shows that the situation should be considered not problematic or alarming.

As this analysis helps us demonstrate, the conflicting aspect of this discussion escalates through the questioning, on both sides, of what the other party proposes. In excerpts #1 and #2, Robert and Marius questioned the way the meetings were currently organized, which led them to propose alternative solutions. These solutions, as we saw, were systematically called into question by the director. In excerpt #3, we see, however, how Marius and Robert then start to question, in their turn, what the director proposes as potential solutions. Each party thus appears to hold its position, which prevents them from moving or progressing toward the negotiation of a middle ground or passage point.

Finding a middle ground would consist, according to speech act theory, in identifying *what in the present circumstances might authorize them to agree on something*. A practice, claim, prediction, proposition, suggestion, or offer is therefore always evaluated on the basis of not only *who*, but also *what* dictates, prescribes, authorizes, or requires it. As we saw, these circumstances can come from the present, but also from the past and even the future, depending on what the interlocutors are led to focus on during the discussion.

If organizing is, as already pointed out, a performance, we can see that *disorganizing* is also something that people literally do. Each attempt made by a party to get organized in a specific way (by proposing something, for instance) appears countered or thwarted by the other, which leads to an impression of status quo. The two parties cannot organize a response to what one of them presents as a problem.

But let us see how the discussion goes on, this time mobilizing the use of conversation analysis and ethnomethodology.

Conversation Analysis/Ethnomethodology

Here is how the conversation progresses.

Excerpt #4

1485	Marius	=But couldn't we [in this case
1486	Director	[But maybe for uh::
1487	Robert	Personally I have never seen that, to have meetings with
1488		everyone and to empty a hospital uh I have never seen that in
1489		any hospital
1490		(0.5)
1491	Director	Well this this takes place uh everywhere↑=

1492	Robert	=I saw meetings uh ((scratching his nose)) every morning uh::
1493		with the department head uh the physicians who are doing their
1494		ward rounds with all the nurses uh present in each ward (.) uh
1495		(0.5) To have meet- meetings uh to empty the services three
1496		times a week uh↑ ((with a tone marking a form of skepticism or
1497		incredulity)) We'll– we'll see uh, but personally I don't have
1498		uh::=
1499	Marius	=Couldn't we also [xxxx
1500	Director	[Yes, this depends on the systems, in fact, uh
1501		Marius and Robert (.) This depends on the system (1.0) and uh
1502		each system has its efficiencies and its uh (.) inefficiencies uh
1503		and now it's up to the service or to the system to see uh:: and to
1504		weigh up uh the pros and the cons.
1505		(.)
1506	Marius	Yes but after there are several solutions, there are several uh
1507	Director	So [either we –
1508	Marius	[reflections to have also [uh=
1509	Director	[Yes
1510	Marius	=For example uh wouldn't the nurse who is on duty and the
1511		department head be already enough↑ (.) This would still allow
1512		all the nurses to attend the meet- the meeting once a week, given
1513		that there will be rotations (.) and therefore that the one who
1514		begins his shift at 8:00 a.m. be indeed on duty (.) That way the
1515		one who has just finished his shift could (.) share his
1516		information about- about what happened during his shift (.) the
1517		problems he had, with the department head, with the doctors,
1518		but at least the one who has just started will be on duty and
1519		working (.) and this– this nurse who is working at that time↑ (.)
1520		will participate in the next meeting. Given that these are
1521		rotations (.) this will never be the same nurses and all the nurses
1522		will participate in the meetings.
1523		(0.5)
1524	Marius	Uh: separately, but at least this– this could also be a solution↑
1525	Director	Well all of these are reflections that we have to carry out uh but
1526		first let's give time to time and observe (.) and maybe we will
1527		have::: to specify that well (.) during such or such period there
1528		were as many crises because we, everything we are talking
1529		about, it's in the abstract= ((movement of his hand on top of his
1530		head))
1531	Marius	Yes=

As we see, the situation does not seem to improve. Marius tries again to make a proposition, but must finally interrupt himself as the director begins to speak at the same time (lines 1485–6). This new impasse then seems to prompt Robert to make a sort of killer statement: "Personally I have never seen that, to have meetings with everyone and to empty a hospital uh I have never seen that in any hospital" (lines 1487–9). After a short pause, which certainly marks a sort of surprise on the director's part, the latter retorts that this kind of meeting actually takes place everywhere (line 1491). Robert then responds by enumerating the type of meetings he already witnessed in other hospitals (lines 1492–4), an enumeration that he contrasts with the present situation in a tone that marks his skepticism or incredulity (lines 1495–7). He then ends his turn of talk by implying that they are ready to wait and see what happens, while reaffirming his reserve ("We'll– we'll see uh, but personally I don't have uh::," lines 1497–8).

Marius then tries to go back with his proposition (line 1499), but is again interrupted by the director who asserts the unique character of each system in what almost sounds like a lesson he is now teaching to his interlocutors (lines 1500–3). Because of this uniqueness, it is therefore, according to him, the system's prerogative "to weigh up uh the pros and the cons" (lines 1503–4) and decide what to do. Marius has not given up and goes back to his proposal, which he is ultimately able to present from lines 1510 to 1522. According to him, the rotation of nurses would allow the latter to attend the meetings each in turn while having one of them on duty on each ward.

The director does not give up either and identifies all the solutions that Marius and Robert proposed as being part of reflections that will have to be carried out later (line 1525). He then proposes to "give time to time" (line 1526) and to observe how many crises will actually take place during the meetings (lines 1527–8), invoking the abstractness of the discussions that have been taking place so far (lines 1529–30).

With conversation analysis/ethnomethodology, we will now focus on the *sequential* aspect of this discussion, that is, how each turn of talk can be analyzed as not only responding to a current

context (what a participant just said, for instance), but also transforming this very context by renaming it or orienting to something
else. In keeping with ethnomethodology's notion of *reflexivity*,
we will also observe how each party attempts to enact and constitute aspects of a situation that can be accepted or not by the
other. Furthermore, this type of analysis will allow us to highlight
the *normative* character of this discussion, a normativity that is
directly associated with its accountable dimension.

If you look back at excerpts 1, 2, and 3, you will note that
Marius and Robert were very careful not to directly question the
way the meetings were organized. In other words, at no point do
we hear them *explicitly* saying that these meetings put the patients
of the hospital at risk and that they should therefore be reconsid-
ered. What they do, however, is account for how the meetings
are presently organized and then highlight the problems that this
generates, according to them. Even if this looks quite similar to
mere criticism, this strategy allows them, as we saw, to let the
facts speak for themselves, that is, it is supposed to let the director
connect the dots, so to speak.

Had they started to say something like, "These meetings are
hazardous because they put the patients of the hospital at risk,"
chances are that the director could have questioned the authority
of their statement, as well as their own authority, that is, what
would authorize them to say that. It would also have *personalized*
the discussion. Orienting to the facts themselves, that is, letting
them speak for themselves, thus allows Marius and Robert to
somehow imply that they are not the ones who claim that these
meetings are dangerous. It is the facts they present and to which
they orient that are supposed to show or demonstrate that something is wrong, something which dictates that some action be
taken to redress this situation. This form of *self-effacement* can
be found, for instance, on lines 1317–19, 1325–32, 1412–15,
1424–6 in the previous excerpts.

Interestingly, the only time Robert speaks about the positive
aspects of the meetings, he does not hesitate to attribute the source
of what is said to himself or Marius. For instance, Robert says, "I
understand very well the idea of having updates, transmissions,

etcetera" (lines 1408–10), as well as "Marius, he says these– these meetings are very good" (line 1412), something that Marius confirms by nodding. In other words, while Marius and Robert make the facts *and only the facts* speak for themselves when it comes to questioning the way these meetings are held, they do not hesitate to highlight that they are the authors of the positive evaluations they also attribute to these meetings. In this case, self-effacement gives way to self-affirmation.

Of course, we and everybody round the table understand that Marius and Robert are calling into question the way these meetings are organized, but *a lot of interactional work is accomplished by the MSF representatives to reflexively deflect the source of the demonstration to the facts that they present while reflexively concentrating the source of praise to themselves*. This allows them to side or align with the director when it comes to affirming the positive aspects of the meetings, while self-effacing when it comes to showing or demonstrating what is wrong with these events. This results in the implicit projection or staging of a "we" composed of the three participants. This "we" values the existence of these meetings, but is supposed to face an "it" made of problems that Marius and Robert are highlighting.

When it comes to making propositions, we also saw how Marius and Robert kept presenting them under the form of questions, which invited the director to react and respond, creating another effect of inclusion. These questions were oriented either to the situation itself ("Wouldn't it be more construct–" (line 1407) "Wouldn't it be more constructive to do that with the department head," lines 1415–16) or to the director (and the personnel he represents) ("Wouldn't you have more constructive discussions," lines 1407–8). On lines 1456–7, a "we" (which is implicitly composed of the three participants) is even staged by Marius when he says, "Yeah but in that case too, we could– we can– we could also think of a rotation of nurses," which also invites the director to react, an invitation that is reiterated on line 1485 in excerpt #4: "But couldn't we in this case."

Despite these numerous attempts to objectify the problems and to include the director in the process of solving them, we also saw how the latter kept marking his disaffiliation through-out the discussion. This disaffiliation is implied either when he orients to other aspects of the situation that, for him, demonstrate the absence of issues or the problematic character of what his interlocutors propose (lines 1322–4, 1333–8, 1419–23, 1442–5, 1447–50), or when he marks his personal attachment to the way the meetings are presently organized ("I think that::: the ideal situation is uh to give the opportunity to everyone (.) to:: be able uh to participate in these meetings (.) and:: to have uh:: uh a – a level that is updated everyday," lines 1431–3).

Similar to Marius and Robert, the director does not hesitate to personalize his attachment, that is, to stage himself in what he says when he talks about his preferences, while *depersonalizing* the source of demonstration when it comes to showing that there is no problem with the present situation, hence the same effects of self-effacement in this case. As we saw, it is therefore as if it were not he who was showing that there was no problem or that the solutions proposed were questionable, but the situation itself. If there is disaffiliation on the director's part, it is so far only marked indirectly through the affirmation of his preferences and the objectivation or factualization of what makes Marius and Robert's propositions problematic.

Again, we and the three participants round the table understand that the director wants to preserve the way the meetings are presently organized, but at no point does the director *explicitly* say, "The way you are presenting the situation is erroneous and your solutions are counterproductive." He lets the facts speak for themselves while reaffirming his own attachment to what currently exists.

His usage of the pronoun "we" is also noteworthy in the previous excerpts. This "we" sometimes does not include Robert and Marius as when he affirms an attachment to the way the meetings are presently organized ("we wish to always stay with everybody," lines 1421–2, and "we always want to have nurses who are versatile," lines 1453–4). This "we" is an exclusive one, which refers to the director and his hospital team. However, there is a more inclusive "we" that includes his interlocutors, as in "because we have to start from the risks that we have already run" (lines 1427–9) or "Well (.) these are uh:: propositions that we cannot::: say yes now (.) This needs to be further pursued uh so uh we always have to start with numbers (.) as you often say (.) so we say that during a period in such and such service there were how many prob-problems while we were at the meeting (.) If we note that::" (lines 1459–63).

If the director marks his relative disaffiliation from Robert and Marius through what he says he and his team prefer, his affiliation with them is also implied when it comes to proposing what the three of them should do, that is, evaluate the risks with numbers. This affiliation is conveyed all the more when he reminds his inter-locutors that they often recommend the same thing ("we always have to start with numbers (.) as you often say," lines 1460–1). While we saw that Robert and Marius included the director by implicitly inviting him to react to their propositions, the director's own strategy of inclusion/affiliation thus seems more explicit or blunt. He does not hesitate to speak in their name when it comes to what they should do.

Having summarized what has happened so far, we can now contrast the first three excerpts with the fourth, which is marked at its beginning by Robert's killer statement ("Personally I have never seen that, to have meetings with everyone and to empty a hospital uh I have never seen that in any hospital," lines 1487–9). Until that point, whenever Marius and Robert highlighted what they considered to be problems with the meetings, we saw that their strategy consisted of presenting facts that were made to speak by themselves. This was a way, as noted, to deflect the source of demonstration to the facts themselves. However, we now see how Robert changes the tone of the discussion by including himself in his strong statement.

By saying that he never saw any other hospital functioning like this, Robert not only highlights the idiosyncratic character of the hospital they are talking about, but also reflexively stages himself as the source of this observation. While the facade of an affilia-tion had been almost artificially maintained until now, this effect of personalization thus establishes a *new context* where Robert now positions himself as the source of the demonstration. This move also amounts to positioning him as a source of authority, an authority that is established through his past experience. In his entire career, he never saw a hospital functioning like this one, a statement that implies that this institution does not function like a normal institution, as it should.

While the director retorts that these types of meeting take place everywhere, Robert continues by invoking again his past experience with hospitals (lines 1492–4), an experience that demonstrates that the way the meetings are presently organized is atypical and therefore abnormal. To the previous sources of authority that Robert and Marius had mobilized, which we saw were mainly factual, Robert now adds one that is more personal: his own experience as an MSF manager. This personalization can also be felt through his tone of skepticism or incredulity when he declares, "To have meet- meetings uh to empty the services three times a week↑ We'll– we'll see uh, but personally I don't have uh::" (lines 1495–6). Although he does not say it explicitly, this tone signals that he is *unconvinced* that this is the right thing to do.

Although mutual disagreement could definitely be felt prior to this episode, it is the first time that one of the participants signals it in such an explicit way, marking a deterioration/polarization of the discussion. Perhaps aware that this might lead them to an impasse, Marius then tries to return to his proposition (line 1499), but is again interrupted by the director, who reacts to what Robert has just said. While we just saw that Robert was personalizing the discussion by invoking his experience, the director adopts a different strategy by speaking to his interlocutors a little condescendingly, as a teacher would speak to his students. He calls them, for instance, by their first names, as if he wanted to gain their attention (line 1501) and then speaks as if he were presenting a general law regarding the way systems work ("This depends on the system (1.0) and uh each system has its efficiencies and its uh (.) inefficiencies uh," lines 1501–2).

Having reminded his interlocutors how a system works, he then tells them that "it's up to the service or to the system to see uh::: and to weigh up uh the pros and the cons" (lines 1503–4), a way to state *who or what is authorized* to make a decision in this kind of situation. While the three participants were essentially orienting to what they presented as facts to support their respective positions, we now see how the director explicitly orients to questions of *rights and obligations*, marking another polarization/deterioration of the discussion. Reminding or telling his interlocutors who or what ultimately decides in this kind of situation also contributes to the personalization of the debate. They are not talking any more about what the best solution might be. *They are now talking about who or what is in charge.*

But Marius has not abandoned his attempt to propose a solution and is finally able to present it from lines 1510 to 1522. With the rotation of nurses that he proposes, "this will never be the same nurses and all the nurses will participate in the meetings" (lines 1521–2). His solution is a priori ideal, since it seems to respond to two opposing concerns: a concern for the sharing of information (the director's) and a concern for the security of the patients (MSF's). After a brief pause, he however goes back to his statement and specifies "Uh: separately, but at least this– this could also be a solution↑" (line 1524).

The director does not seem very impressed and redefines the solutions that Marius and Robert proposed as *reflections* that they will have to carry out later (line 1525). While a solution could result in a series of decisions and interventions that would change the way the meetings are organized, a reflection presupposes that the solution is yet to be found and, as the director says, that they have to "give time to time" (line 1526). To a context of intervention, the director responds with a context of reflection and verification. As he says, they need to check how many crises will actually take place during the meetings (lines 1527–8), which reiterates the idea of getting the numbers in order to identify what the situation really looks like regarding these meetings.

To the concreteness of the numbers, he then opposes the abstractness of the discussion that, according to him, they have been having so far (lines 1528–9). From the rights and obligations of the participants, we now reach the level of the conversation itself, which becomes an object of discussion.

As conversation analysis allows us to show, this discussion about the hospital meetings appears to evolve in terms of what is oriented to and invoked by the participants. Although it was clear from the beginning that both parties disagreed about what to do regarding these meetings, we saw that a lot of interactional work was done, during the first three excerpts, to deflect the source of their respective demonstrations to the facts and principles they were presenting. These facts and principles were portrayed as speaking for themselves, that is, showing or demonstrating that the way these meetings were organized had to be changed or maintained. In contrast, these effects of depersonalization were balanced by effects of personalization when the two parties were reaffirming their attachment to the *raison d'être* of these meetings, a move that allowed them to affiliate and identify with each other regarding this question.

We saw, however, how the discussion quickly deteriorated in the fourth excerpt. First, when Robert explicitly marked his disaffiliation/disalignment from the director's position, and, second, when the director himself started to talk about the parties' rights and obligations. These two moves marked a personalization of the discussion: participants were not talking about facts or principles that supported or not their respective positions; they now marked their explicit disagreement and spoke about who was allowed to do what in the present situation. The context of the discussion then reflexively changed through the various turns of talk we analyzed. A polarization thus took place through the affirmation of their disagreement, which had remained implicit until then.

In terms of accountability, the normative character of the discussion also evolved toward more personalization. In the first three excerpts, it was the facts and principles presented by both parties that were supposed to dictate, require, or demand that some action be taken or not. In the fourth excerpt, however, this source can now be found in Robert's personal experience or in the participants' rights and obligations. In other words, we observe a *shift* from *what* to *who* dictates what should be done about the reunions. The opposition is not just between facts and principles, but also between two parties who now mark their explicit disagreement with each other.

As we will see, this shift will be confirmed by what narrative analysis can tell us about what follows just after.

Narrative Analysis

Excerpt #5

1532	Director	=It's [just to allow us to get there
1533	Marius	[Yes, but no ((with an irritated tone and face)) but still we
1534		are doing medical work↑ we try to have uh to reach objectives uh
1535		of quality at the level of healthcare=
1536	Director	=Well=
1537	Marius	= And to say, "We wait (.) we wait until there is a problem to
1538		change things" (.) personally this:: bothers me a little this type of
1539		reflection.
1540		(0.5)
1541	Director	No=
1542	Marius	=So=
1543	Director	=It's not that this bothers you, but uh let's give time to time and
1544		follow up (.) [uh and::
1545	Marius	[This means that we are going to wait until there is a
1546		problem, until there is someone dead in a ward to say, "Ah, it's
1547		true it's not good and now we have to change."
1548		(0.5)
1549	Director	Hhh ((chuckling uneasily while looking at his papers on the
1550		desk))
1551	Marius	Personally, this bothers me to:::: to wait until this moment and
1552		avoid- and if we can avoid precisely having someone dead
1553		because uh there is no personnel (.) and that we have solutions
1554		before that can be set up (.) I (.) think that it is better to set them
1555		up before.
1556		(0.5)
1557	Robert	We could discuss [this again too and
1558	Director	[Well maybe we [will-
1559	Robert	[Maybe during an upcoming
1560		meeting uh::
1561	Marius	Yeah

1562	Robert	One of these days ((looking at Marius)) one of these mornings
1563	Marius	Hum
1564	Robert	Uh we could discuss again with the people in each ward with all
1565		the nurses how they see things too↑ uh::
1566	Director	As for uh:: This is uh:: As I say it once again uh:: what I noticed,
1567		it is that <u>sometimes</u> (.) there are people who come in between and
1568		give orders ((moving his hand toward Marius while looking at
1569		him intently)) here and there (.) and somehow this perturbs the
1570		system.
1571		(1.0)
1572	Director	Uh decisions (.) must leave from one point (.) to go uh[::
1573	Marius	[Ah this is
1574		why [we have been discussing this morning uh
1575	Director	[In different services
1576	Marius	This is why we are discussing this morning
1577		(0.5)
1578	Marius	[To get to an agreement
1579	Director	[So we are the same and if there are things to be discussed, we
1580		discuss and then well, we settle on something and we give lines
1581		of conduct to others=
1582	Marius	=Of course, yes=
1583	Director	=Because in each system, there is uh the conception and the
1584		execution. And the conception, this is all the meetings and
1585		discussions that we have, and the execution, now, it's:: very
1586		heavy↑
1587	Marius	Ah but this is what we are doing this morning. This is why–
1588		((chuckling with a big smile))

As we see, the discussion continues to deteriorate as Marius interrupts the director to explicitly voice his irritation about the whole situation (lines 1533–5). While the discussion had so far focused on the meetings as well as the way this hospital and others function, we see him reminding the director about what they are here to do ("but still we are doing medical work↑," lines 1533–40) and what their ultimate mission is ("we try to have uh to reach objectives uh of quality at the level of healthcare," lines 1534–5). He then paraphrases what the director just said without mentioning that it is the latter who pronounced these words, as if to mitigate the attack ("And to say, 'We wait (.) we wait until there is a problem to change things,'" lines 1537–8), and declare his opposition to this view ("personally this:: bothers me a little this type of reflection," lines 1538–9).

After a brief pause that could mark an embarrassment on the director's part, the latter responds by saying, "It's not that this bothers you" (line 1543), as if to deny the irritation that Marius has just been voicing and displaying. He then reiterates his position ("but uh let's give time to time and follow up (.) uh and::" (lines 1543–4), which prompts Marius to explain what could be, for him, the consequences of this wait-and-see attitude ("This means that we are going to wait until there is a problem, until there is someone dead in a ward to say, 'Ah, it's true it's not good and now we have to change,'" lines 1545–7).

As the director's embarrassment continues to be felt (he chuckles uneasily while looking at his papers on the desk, lines 1549–50), Marius again reaffirms his disapproval ("Personally, this bothers me to:::: to wait until this moment," line 1551) and the necessity to do something before someone dies in the hospital ("if we can avoid precisely having someone dead because uh there is no personnel (.) and that we have solutions before that can be set up (.) I (.) think that it is better to set them up before," lines 1552–5).

As if to break the tension that is now clearly palpable between the two men, Robert intervenes by proposing to postpone the discussion to another occasion ("We could discuss this again too and ... maybe during an upcoming meeting," lines 1557–60), a solution to which the director seems to align ("Well maybe we will," line 1558). Marius having also marked his own alignment ("Yeah," 1561), Robert specifies when this discussion could take place ("One of these days ((looking at Marius)) one of these mornings," line 1562) and with whom ("Uh we could discuss again with the people in each ward with all the nurses how they see things too↑ uh::," lines 1564–5).

This mention of the opening of the discussion to other people does not seem, however, to please the director as he declares: "As for uh:: This is uh:: As I say it once again uh:: what I noticed, it is that <u>sometimes</u> (.) there are people who come in between and give orders ((moving his hand toward Marius while looking at him intently)) here and there (.) and somehow this perturbs the system (1.0) Uh decisions (.) must leave from one point (.) to go uh ... in different services" (lines 1566–75). Although he never specifies who these people are, the allusion to Marius is clear as he moves his hand toward the latter while looking at him. What appears to be a call to order also implies that the democratic move Robert just proposed would amount, according to the director, to questioning the chain of command, that is, his own authority as the director of the hospital.

Reacting to this implicit critique, Marius responds, "Ah this is why we discussed this morning uh. This is why we are discussing this morning (0.5) To get an agreement" (lines 1573–8), a response that is supposed to show that what they are presently doing, having this meeting, is meant to precisely allow decisions to come from one point, that is, from the hospital management. In other words, the director's preoccupations regarding the way this hospital should function are presented by Marius as also being theirs, that is, Marius's and Robert's.

The director then reaffirms this agreement they seem to be having and takes the opportunity to define how things should work regarding decision-making processes in his hospital ("So we are the same and if there are things to be discussed, we discuss and then well, we settle on something and we give lines of conducts to others," lines 1579–81). After Marius marks his alignment to this position (line 1582), the director then reiterates it through what now sounds again like a management class he would be teaching to his interlocutors, a teaching tainted, however, by reproaches: "Because in each system, there is uh the conception and the execution. And the conception, this is all the meetings and discussions that we have, and the execution, now, it's:: very heavy↑" (lines 1583–6).

So let's now see what a narrative analysis could help us observe and unveil in this excerpt. As we already know with Bruner (1991), narratives are characterized by specific features, in particular their *diachronicity*, that is, the fact that they are composed of events that occur over time. They are also characterized by their *context sensibility and negotiability*, which means that they should always be considered perspectives on specific situations. The way a story is told regarding a situation will therefore always depend on which events and characters are *selected* and how they are *defined*.

Although Marius, Robert, and the director do not explicitly tell stories in this specific part of the meeting, they often present what is taking place in their discussion as being in contrast or alignment with other things that have already happened in the past or should happen in the future. In other words, they include the present discussion in a process that appears to supersede it, giving it a specific sense, interpretation, or meaning. This is the kind of narrative mechanism that we will focus on, since it shows *how the narrating of events constitutes and participates in the polemical dimension of this discussion*.

In the beginning of the excerpt, we see, for instance, how Marius creates a contrast with the director's wait-and-see attitude by reminding the director what their mission is supposed to be about, which is to say, doing medical work and trying to reach objectives of quality in healthcare (lines 1533–5). The director and his attitude are implicitly presented as *obstacles* vis-à-vis MSF's and the hospital's mission. There is, in other words, a *breach*: the canonical scripts of the hospital and the humanitarian organization are presented as violated or infringed by the director himself. In this implicit story that is told, Marius thus positions himself as a subject/hero trying to fulfill his noble mission, a mission that we all understand is thwarted by his interlocutor, hence his frustration, which can be clearly felt throughout this discussion.

If the narrative that Marius implicitly mobilizes orients to the ongoing mission, it also evokes events that might happen in the future (lines 1545–6), events where patients would die because of what the director proposes to do. We even see him staging a situation where people would be led to say: "Ah it's true it's not good and now we have to change" (lines 1546–7), as if to reinforce the surreal aspect of the situation. Marius thus projects a bleak future presented as a consequence of the decision to adopt a wait-and-see attitude. Having established this narrative path, he reminds his interlocutor that they have "solutions before that can be set up" (lines 1553–4), which would thus offer another direction in what is implicitly presented as a crossroads in this discussion.

Interestingly, this narrativization of the situation also illustrates the personalization/radicalization of the conflict between the two men, a personalization/radicalization that was noted before and that progressively rose throughout the discussion. While the first four excerpts staged three people who positioned themselves as searching for a solution vis-à-vis the question of the meetings, Marius now implicitly presents himself as a subject/hero confronting an anti-subject/villain, impersonated by the director. Constitutively speaking, it is therefore as if a shift had taken place in terms of how the situation is presented: *from a situation/ narrative of apparent collaboration to a situation/narrative of confrontation.*

Even if this confrontation of viewpoints could be felt throughout the first four excerpts, it had so far not been voiced as explicitly as it is now. As shown previously, a facade of collaboration had indeed been interactively maintained or worked out by the three protagonists, positioning them as trying to solve a problem, either by proposing alternative forms of meetings (Marius and Robert) or by negating the existence of the said problem and proposing to wait and see what would happen (the director). The shift that we observe thus consists of making explicit what had so far remained implicit or relatively silent. The director's attitude "bothers" (lines 1538 and 1551) Marius and the latter explains why: the director's solution is not a solution, since it consists of maintaining the status quo and paving the way to a lethal incident.

As mentioned before, we can speculate that Robert, who is Marius's supervisor, realizes that this radicalization takes them nowhere (after all, they have no choice but to collaborate), which leads him to offer to postpone the present discussion (line 1557). This move thus consists of reinserting what is happening in a narrative of collaboration, since the debate they are having is now implicitly redefined as participating in a series of discussions, which could happen "one of these mornings" (line 1562). Robert even extends this idea of collaboration to other participants – "the people in each ward with all the nurses" (lines 1564–5) – as if to imply that this problem-solving process should be participative and open to other members of the hospital.

To Marius's narrative of confrontation, Robert thus responds with a narrative of integration and participation: all the people who are concerned with what is presently debated should be involved in this discussion so that they can tell them "how they see things too" (line 1565). In this narrative, everybody, including the director, is positioned as a subject facing the same problem to be solved. However, it is also a situation where the director's voice, despite its formal authority, could, of course, be positioned as one among others. In other words, Robert's solution could be seen as a way to dilute and weaken the director's position, if this one proves to be in minority.

The director seems to understand what is at stake in this move as he reacts to what Robert just said by telling another story of his own, which is presented as having been already recounted ("As I say it once again," line 1566). In this story, we see "people" (who are not named) "who come in between and give orders here and there" (lines 1567–9), a situation that "somehow ... perturbs the system" (lines 1569–70). As in any good narrative, the director's story thus stages opponents, villains, or anti-subjects whose actions upset, trouble, or disturb the established order. Although these people are not identified, the director does not fail to look at Marius intently while evoking this situation. One of the people he is talking about clearly seems to be right in front of him ...

And as in any good story, there is, of course, a moral, which is supposed to teach us what should be done in this kind of situation: "Uh decisions (.) must leave from one point to go uh:: in different services" (lines 1572–5). Opening the problem-solving process to more people (which is what Robert proposes to do) would amount, according to the director, to doing what Marius tends to do too often in the hospital, that is, perturbing the system by intervening here and there while shortcutting the hierarchical structure. To Robert's narrative of integration and participation, the director thus responds with a *narrative of command and control*: decisions need to come from one point (his point) and be communicated to the services. No need, therefore, to involve the services in the decision-making process.

Interestingly, Marius immediately reacts by telling the director that this is why they have been discussing this morning (lines 1573–4, 1576). In other words, the whole discussion can be considered part of the narrative of command and control that the director just put forward. But this move could also be understood as a way to tell the director that their narrative of collaboration is, in fact, compatible with his narrative of centralism: collaborating or cooperating with you, which is what we are doing now, is a way to make sure that we are on the same wavelength and that the decisions can then be communicated from one point to the services. No mention is made, however, of the narrative of participation, which remains a priori incompatible with what the director has just put forward.

The director then acknowledges this form of alignment (line 1579) and reaffirms his position by now redefining the discussions they are having and will have through his command-and-control narrative: "If there are things to be discussed, we discuss and then well, we settle on something and we give line of conducts to others" (lines 1579–81). In other words, we discuss, we collaborate, but then we make a decision at some point and tell others what to do. A key part of this reminder is "we settle on something," meaning that once a decision is made, the discussion is over and Marius (and other people) cannot come in between and ultimately question what has been agreed on. Others' participation is, at this level, not an option.

After Marius marks his agreement (line 1582), the director reiterates his position, but this time through the form of a general law under which the discussions they are having and will have are subsumed: "Because in each system, there is uh the conception and the execution. And the conception, this is all the meetings and discussion that we have, and the execution, now, it's:: very heavy" (lines 1583–6). The narrative of command and control is therefore reaffirmed through the form of its moral, a moral that the director presents as a general law of management.

The reference to this law also allows him to allude, once more, to the problem of execution he is having, implying that Marius (and possibly other people) interfere with it. In the director's narrative, it is these people who are the anti-subjects, obstacles, or opponents to the hierarchical order he is promoting.

As this analysis shows, the conflict between the three men tends to *exist more or less* depending on which narrative they choose to tell. As long as the narrative of collaboration is implicitly told – a narrative where each protagonist was presenting himself or positioned as trying to find a solution to the meetings problem – this way of presenting the situation could work as a facade vis-à-vis the tensions that could be felt throughout the first four excerpts. However, we saw how alternate narratives started to be recounted in excerpt 5, especially a narrative of confrontation where the director was positioned as an opponent or obstacle vis-à-vis MSF's and the hospital's missions.

We also saw how the director responded to this attack by telling a narrative of his own, a narrative of command and control where Marius and others were positioned as opponents or obstacles vis-à-vis the hierarchical line. While a certain polarization could be implicitly felt throughout the first four excerpts, the fifth excerpt gives it an explicit existence. The conflict is now *narrated into being*, so to speak, with hero, missions, opponents, morals, and possible resolutions. Its mode of existence thus augments, since it exists not only in the gaze and intonation of the participants and in their implicit rejections of each other's ideas, but also in the way each person is now defined.

But if this conflict now becomes more explicit, we also saw how both parties tried to counterbalance it by retelling a tale of collaboration, a tale where everyone seems ultimately ready to cooperate despite the divisions. At least two narratives thus coexist and compete with each other throughout this episode, two ways of making sense of the situation: a way where the protagonists are cooperating to find solutions to problems that have been exposed and a way where they orient to each other as opponents or obstacles vis-à-vis this resolution. These two narratives exist more or less depending on the moment of the discussion.

So let's see now how this whole affair tentatively ends, mobilizing the sixth perspective, critical discourse analysis.

Critical Discourse Analysis

Excerpt #6

1589	Director	It's a reflection↑ We're gonna see because there are several
1590		alternatives uh Should we start uh:: letting the head of the
1591		department and the physicians together, should we- which nurse
1592		stays and which arrives, should we, we should, it's really a reflection
1593		that remains uh[::: xxx
1594	Robert	[I think we should broaden the discussion uh:: not
1595		only between us ((smiling)) so that we can discuss with other
1596		physicians and the department heads=
1597	Marius	=I know that it is already Gerald who told me. It's a physician who
1598		thinks that these meetings are interesting but (0.5) that is:: that we
1599		are taking risks (.) that- that we could really avoid emptying the
1600		wards with the nursing staff, with the whole nursing staff ((with a
1601		grave face))
1602		(1.0)
1603	Director	Well the reflections uh::::: they could take one, two or three days, but
1604		these are reflections and after we settle on a system that is uh
1605		effective instead of saying straightaway, "Well, we take– We leave a
1606		nurse, then we do this"
1607	Robert	[No no=
1608	Marius	[No no
1609	Robert	=But we are not saying that for tomorrow morning=
1610	Marius	=No [exactly, exactly
1611	Robert	[It's exactly what we are saying. We discuss that, during the
1612		next meeting on Monday morning, maybe we discuss this with that
1613		team. On Wednesday, we discuss this again and then we see what
1614		people think about it too
1615	Marius	What we are thinking about is a short-term reflection ((chuckling
1616		with a big smile addressed to the director))
1617		(2.0)
1618	Director	Okay, I don't know if you are done, but there are people coming
1619		from Kinshasa too
1620	Marius	No, [it's good
1621	Director	[with whom we have to speak

Again, we see how the director reframes the whole discussion that took place as "a reflection" (lines 1589 and 1592). While Robert and Marius have been pushing for a quick decision regarding the meetings, the director reaffirms the deliberative character of the present reunion: they are not here to make a decision, but to reflect collectively on what to do about this question. The decision is therefore implicitly postponed by the director ("We're gonna see," line 1589) because various alternatives are supposed to present themselves to them, which force them to reflect on the situation with a clear head (lines 1589–90). Picking up on this idea of reflection, Robert then takes the opportunity to put forward again his own idea of broadening the discussion to other people, especially physicians and department heads (lines 1594–6).

Robert's proposal is echoed by Marius, who reproduces something that a physician (called Gerald) told him about the risks they are running with these meetings (lines 1597–1601). We then see the director indirectly reacting to what Robert and Marius just said by reaffirming that these are reflections that could take up to three days. The physicians, the department heads, or anyone else could give their opinion about the meetings, but "after we settle on a system that is uh effective instead of saying straightaway, 'Well, we take- we leave a nurse, then we do this'" (lines 1604–6). The decision should therefore not be hurried and is their prerogative.

A sort of compromise thus seems to emerge as the director appears to accept the idea that other people could give their opinion while reaffirming that these opinions are just reflections that will ultimately lead to a decision that they – the director and MSF – will take in two or three days. Robert and Marius then immediately jump on this opening by assuring the director that they were not thinking of a decision that would be implemented instantly ("But we are not saying that for tomorrow morning," line 1609). Robert then specifies what these reflections might look like over the next three days (lines 1611–14), a description that Marius, wearing a big smile, punctuates by telling the director what their expectations actually are ("What we are thinking about is a short-term reflection," lines 1615–16), as if to imply that reflections can often take a long time in this hospital.

The discussion ends (for now) on this compromise as the director asks Marius and Robert if they are done with their business, on the pretext that he needs to speak to people coming from Kinshasa, the capital city (lines 1618–19). Marius then responds, "It's good," which closes the conversation.

So what can critical discourse analysis say about this final excerpt as well as the whole discussion about the meetings? First, it is important to remember that critical scholars are interested in *power relationships*, which leads them to analyze any interaction not only in terms of what people are telling each other, but also in terms of what kinds of discourse/ideologies tend to be reproduced through specific interactions. As Foucault (1981, 1984) pointed out, people are bearers of specific regimes of truth that can oppose or conflict with each other in a given situation. When people talk, write, or, more generally, communicate, they tend to represent, embody, or materialize these different orders of discourse, which participate in the reproduction, alteration, or transformation of social practices (Fairclough, 2005).

A critical scholar would then focus not only on what the director, Marius, and Robert are telling each other in this specific reunion, but also on its context or circumstances. As pointed out before, a critical perspective indeed tends to be interested in the *conditions of possibility* of a specific interaction or discourse, that is, in what makes it possible not only in terms of what is said and how it is said, but also in terms of *who* is authorized or compelled to say what is said and what authorizes or constrains the protagonists to say what they say.

In the case of our meeting, we already saw that Marius and Robert are MSF representatives, with Robert being officially Marius's boss. Both of them are young, white expatriates and managers. Although they work for Doctors Without Borders, they are not physicians themselves. This is quite common for a humanitarian organization such as MSF, given the importance logistics and management have for this organization. As for the director, he is a physician from the Democratic Republic of the Congo. He is black, a little older than his interlocutors, and, as a director of his institution, also represents the regional government of his country.

In terms of relations of power, both parties know that, beyond their disagreements, they have to work with each other. MSF comes, of course, with a lot of resources (equipment, money, nurses, doctors, logisticians, etc.) and is officially supporting the hospital. What this concretely means is that the salaries of the hospital staff will sometimes more than double, while the hospital itself will suddenly benefit from new equipment and drugs they could not get otherwise, as well as physicians and nurses who volunteer for MSF and will complement the local personnel already present.

As we see, while we can talk about support, the new conditions implemented in the hospital are such that we could easily claim that MSF is almost *taking over* this institution: new procedures, new methods, and new staff are implemented in this hospital. However, MSF also knows that they have to *cooperate* with the representatives of the hospital, since the last thing they want is to appear like a sort of neocolonial organization that would impose its standards, its personnel, and its practices (after all, if they are in the DRC, it is also because the government agrees to let them in). Even if this is, to some extent, a postcolonial situation, a lot of collaboration takes place, on a day-to-day basis, to have the hospital director participate in the decision-making processes.

According to a protocol that both MSF and the hospital representatives signed, decisions have indeed to be made by both parties, which means that they have to collaborate or cooperate, whether they like it or not. The director seems to understand this situation very well, as we saw that he implicitly kept reaffirming his authority throughout the conversation. How does he do that? By systematically questioning what Robert and Marius propose to do regarding the weekly meetings (and this opposition can also be felt in other excerpts that I cannot, unfortunately, reproduce in this chapter for lack of space).

This knowledge of the context is important to understand why we were able to observe three phases in this conversation. A *first phase* corresponds with the sequence during which Robert and Marius keep proposing solutions to what they consider to be problem of the meetings, while the director keeps responding that there is no problem with these meetings or that the solutions his interlocutors are proposing are unpractical or counterproductive. I propose to name this first phase, which roughly corresponds with excerpts 1, 2, and 3, a phase of *collaboration*. At least on the surface of the discussion, both parties are indeed trying to figure out *what the situation dictates*, even if we can already see that the director is systematically questioning what his interlocutors propose or claim.

A *second phase* – which corresponds with excerpts 4 and 5 and which I propose to call a phase of *confrontation* – then follows when Robert suddenly says, "Personally I have never seen that, to have meetings with everyone and to empty a hospital uh I have never seen that in any hospital" (lines 1487–9). As we already observed, this second phase is, in a way, already present in the first phase, but it suddenly becomes more explicit or blatant with these two lines of the transcript. How does it become so? Because Robert starts to speak about his own experience, a personalization of the discussion that is presented as contradicting the system of meetings that the director has been defending.

This confrontation continues with Marius, who also becomes personal from lines 1533 to 1555, but then ends when Robert finally says, as to temper the discussion, "We could discuss this again too and" (line 1557). What we then observe is the beginning of a *third phase*, which corresponds with the end of excerpt 5 and the whole of excerpt 6 and could be also called a *phase of collaboration*. During this phase, the three men start to find a way out from confrontation and a way back to compromise. Why is it so? Because both Marius and Robert know that they cannot afford to alienate their interlocutor. They need him as much as he needs them.

Throughout these six excerpts, an opposition – which is, as we saw, more or less overt, explicit, or blatant – can thus be felt between two ways of conceiving what should be done, what we could call *two regimes of truth* or *ideologies*. While this opposition could definitely be felt until Robert's declaration on lines 1487–9, it had not been spelled out before then. What do these two ideologies or regimes of truth look like? For MSF, we could roughly gloss their ideology as "Everything should be done to assure the quality of the patients' healthcare." Interestingly, it is this principle that is implicitly put forward by Marius himself when he also starts to personalize the discussion in excerpt 5 ("Yes, but no ((with an irritated tone and face)) but still we are doing medical work↑ we try to have uh to reach objectives uh of quality at the level of healthcare," lines 1533–5).

We see that Marius talks about what they do or should do ("we are doing medical work") and what their objectives are or should be ("reach objectives uh of quality at the level of healthcare"), which shows that the discussion has now moved to the *raison d'être* of their action. Both he and Robert are still talking about what the situation dictates, but this situation now involves their beliefs, experiences, and missions. It is becoming explicitly personal, which adds, as we saw, to the polarization of the conversation.

As for the director, his regime of truth or ideology could be glossed as "Everything should be done to protect the hospital's system of authority." This principle can actually be heard when he says in excerpt 5, "Because in each system, there is uh the conception and the execution. And the conception, this is all the meetings and discussions that we have, and the execution, now, it's:: very heavy" (lines 1583–6). In a way, the director's opposition, which could be felt from the very beginning of the discussion, can be understood as a way to reaffirm his own authority and the authority of the hospital vis-à-vis MSF.

Given the power balance between the two parties, such an interpretation makes a lot of sense: on one side, one of the biggest humanitarian organizations in the world, with plenty of financial resources, personnel, and equipment, and on the other side, a local hospital from the Democratic Republic of the Congo with very limited means at its disposal. Using Fairclough's (1992, 1995, 2005) terminology, we see that the discussion between the two parties can be analyzed not only as (1) *a text*, that is, everything that is said during this discussion, but also as (2) *a discursive practice*, which corresponds with how this text is produced and interpreted by the parties in presence, and finally as (3) *a social practice*, which corresponds with the political, organizational, cultural, or ideological dimension of this interaction.

It is the analysis of this third dimension of discourse that is the most important for a critical perspective, as it shows *the extent to which discourse contributes to reproducing or altering specific ideological, organizational, cultural, and political structures*. In the case that interests us, we see that this conversation between these three men is not only a discussion between MSF and a local hospital, but also between at least two ideologies or regimes of truth, which we identified. Furthermore, we also understand how this discussion participates in the balance of power between the two organizations. The (dormant or overt) confrontation between the two parties can thus be analyzed as one party – the hospital – trying to counter what is perceived as MSF's attempt to *take it over*.

Critical theorists could even go one step further and analyze this whole discussion as having neocolonialist overtones. In terms of constitution, it is not only MSF that is, for all practical purposes, taking over a local hospital of the Democratic Republic of the Congo, but also an international organization, embodied and represented by two young white men speaking to a black man who is older than them. Furthermore, these two white men are, as I indicated earlier, not physicians, making their interventions all the more problematic in that they consist in telling a director and physician how to run his hospital.

The whole scene could therefore be seen as an attempt, on MSF's part, to impose an occidental way of conceiving of healthcare. According to such a conception, nurses must always be present in the hospital services, leaving no role for the parents and relatives, who usually are at the patients' bedside. While, according to the director, these parents and relatives are supposed to warn the personnel when there is a problem, MSF considers that such a delegation is risky and does not meet their healthcare standards.

We thus see how this whole discussion has important political, organizational, cultural, or ideological dimensions. It is not only three men who meet with each other, but also two worldviews that collide while trying to work with each other.

6

By Way of a Conclusion

What differentiates these discursive perspectives from other approaches to organizational life is, as we now realize, that they focus on *how people communicate with each other*, which means that we have often to dwell on the details of what they are talking about in order to understand the constitutive power of their communicative acts. Although these perspectives could be easily accused of myopia, that is, an inability to see beyond the details of what people say, write, and do, we also saw that communication does not have to be reduced to the *here and now* of a given conversation. In their own specific way, each perspective indeed allowed us to show that *many other things say things* when people communicate with each other.[1]

Defending a constitutive view of communication thus means that *people are not alone on the construction site when they communicate*. Through their turns of talk, situations, circumstances, or facts dictate their future; organizations, administrations, or groups take specific stands; values, ideologies, or principles express themselves; policies, rules, or plans require that action be taken. As we saw, this does not mean that people should be reduced to mere intermediaries or puppets in this picture. They have, on the contrary, always *their own way* of making these things speak, which explains why we observe disagreements or divergences regarding what, for instance, a situation dictates, as exemplified especially in chapter 5.

Defending a constitutive view of communication does not mean that everything starts from communication. It means, on the contrary, that *there is no starting point* and that people should be considered as much *actors* as *passers* when interactions take place. Actors because they actively *participate in* the constitution of their (organizational and social) world, passers because through their actions, others things express themselves (cultures, associations, protocols, norms, etc.) and therefore participate in this constitution. Communication is thus rather an obligatory passage point, that is, the essential means by which societies, organizations, and groups reproduce and transform themselves for another next first time.

As Latour (2013) reminds us, our world is a plural world, but it is also, as Taylor and Van Every (2011, 2014) acutely show us, a world where identities and unities have to be constantly reworked and reaffirmed. It is therefore both one and many (Cooren, Taylor, and Van Every, 2006; Robichaud, Giroux, and Taylor, 2004) and this is why indepth studies of communication are so crucial. Communication is this never-ending process by which our (social, organizational, physical) world, in all its incarnations, materializations, and embodiments, is constantly *relating to itself*, marking both its identity/unity and alteration/alienation. It is a world of alignments, configurations, authorities, and affiliations, but also of confrontations, alienations, subversions, and separations.

If things get organized in a specific way, it is, as we saw, always at the expense of other pathways that could have been taken: traditional staff meetings that now appear to some as counterproductive or even dangerous (chapter 5), a romantic relationship that seems to divert an employee from his duties as a teammate (chapter 4), or any other activities that could be deemed as infringing with what has to be done collectively (chapter 3). The organizational world is, by definition, an alienating world, but it is also a world of cooperation and co-construction. Organizing is always at the price of disorganizing (a meeting, a relationship, other potential activities), hence its polemical dimension.

Notes

Chapter 1 What is (Organizational) Discourse? How is This Book Organized?

1 For more development about the discourse/Discourse distinction, see Alvesson and Kärreman (2011a, 2011b); Bargiela-Chiappini (2011); Hardy and Grant (2012); Iedema (2011); and Mumby (2011).
2 A proxemic feature refers to anything related to the spatial distance between individuals, i.e., what this distance communicates in terms, for instance, of status, relationship, or culture (see Hall, 1966).
3 Of course, when people write to each other, either through the Internet or snail mail, all these non-verbal aspects tend to disappear (but note that emoticons like ☺ or ☹ have precisely been invented to compensate for this lack of information about how we should take what is said).
4 Of course, this tale has its limits in terms of analogy. First, it implies that I have a privileged access to what organizational discourse is, since I would be the only one who is not blind in this story. To clarify this: I am as blind as the others, so just see me as one blind person speaking of other blind persons (but wait, you too would then be blind as well!). Second, and this point is related to the first, this analogy implies that there might be a way to reconcile all these various perspectives (just by telling them what organizational discourse *really* is), which is, of course, illusory. What still makes this tale interesting, I think, is the fact that all the blind men are speaking about the same thing (the elephant), even if they disagree about what this thing is or does.

Chapter 2 Analyzing Organizational Discourse: Six Perspectives

1 This is why rhetoricians tend to be mainly interested in formal speeches or documents as these public performances or texts have sometimes been meticulously crafted and designed to produce specific effects.

2 Where scientists and rhetoricians tend to disagree concerns the way we can control how a fact speaks or what it says. Latour (1987) shows convincingly how scientists are very good at designing and using devices, methodologies, or machines that will make the facts speak in a specific way, making their rhetoric stronger. For instance, European physicists have apparently identified neutrinos that are breaking what is considered the cosmic speed limit, i.e., the speed of light. This result, which seems to contradict one of the most fundamental laws of physics, has, of course, to be confirmed, which means that other experiments will have to be launched in order to check that it is not a mistake, making the evidence of this fact stronger and stronger. Also, should this fact be confirmed, what will remain to be defined is *what it means*, i.e., what *it tells us* about physics, a question that might trigger scientific controversies. Even at this point, scientists would say that they can control how facts speak, since these kinds of scientific controversies might lie on various interpretations of physics, but then rhetoricians would point out that the mere existence of scientific controversies proves that persuasion and argumentation is at stake, which confirms the salience of their viewpoint.

3 Austin's William James Lectures were posthumously edited in 1962 with the title *How To Do Things with Words*. He died in 1960 at age 48.

4 For more details on these transcribing conventions, see Van Dijk (1997a: 312–14), as well as Atkinson and Heritage (1984: ix–xvi).

5 Note that in French, interpellation often has a negative connotation, especially when one speaks of *someone* interpellating someone else. It is typically a person of authority (a policeman, for instance) who interpellates someone else and this interpellation implies that the person interpellated might have done something wrong or is a suspect. In French, this negative connotation tends to disappear, however, when one speaks of *something* that interpellated someone, which then means something that intrigues someone or raises her interest. This negative connotation does not exist systematically in English. For instance, someone could be hailing his friend in the street just to say hello.

Chapter 3 Coordination and Organizing

1 By "incarnatedly," I mean that the existence of, say, a group has to be embodied through specific actions, artifacts, words, principles, representatives, ideas, etc. In other words, it means that it always exists through specific *beings* that are supposed to make it present, to give it a flesh, to actualize it.

2 But even then, we could imagine that it would have been appropriate for Amy to wait until Julia asks her how she was envisaging the division of labor.

Chapter 4 Organizational Culture, Identity, and Ideology

1 From a *differentiation* perspective, organizations, according to Martin (2001), are characterized by the existence of subcultures that coexist and can get into conflict with each other. From a *fragmentation* perspective, cultures are marked by their intrinsic ambiguity, which means that any meaning attached to a practice or habit actually differs from one member to another. Finally, the *integration* perspective highlights the consensual aspect of organizational culture (without an "s").

2 See, for instance, Bruner (1991, 2003); Fisher (1984, 1985, 1989); Robichaud (2003); Taylor and Van Every (2000); and Weick (1995).

3 Here, it is noteworthy that by using the term "discourse," Mumby (1997) is referring to the *academic discourse* itself, and not the discourse that these academics are studying when they analyze texts or people speaking to each other. Mumby distinguishes between four types of discourse: what he calls (1) a discourse of representation, which he associates with positivist modernism; (2) a discourse of understanding, which he associates with interpretivist modernism; (3) a discourse of suspicion, which he associates with critical modernism; and (4) a discourse of vulnerability, which he associates with postmodernism. All these discourses represent various academic conceptions and epistemologies.

Chapter 6 By Way of a Conclusion

1 This is what I proposed to call elsewhere an activity of *ventriloquism* (Cooren, 2010, 2012) in reference to the art by which a person makes a puppet say things in front of an audience. We saw, for instance, how organizational members were able to ventriloquize not only values, ideologies, and principles, but also organizations, policies, facts, or situations (that is, make them say things) when they talk to each other.

References

Albert, S., and Whetten, D. A. (1985). Organizational identity. *Research in Organizational Behavior* 7: 263–95.

Althusser, L. (1971). Ideology and ideological state apparatuses. In *Lenin and Philosophy and Other Essays*. London: Monthly Review Press, pp. 127–86.

Alvesson, M. (2002). *Understanding Organizational Culture*. Thousand Oaks, CA: Sage.

Alvesson, M. (2004). Organizational culture and discourse. In D. Grant, C. Hardy, C. Oswick, and L. L. Putnam (eds), *The Sage Handbook of Organizational Discourse*. London: Sage, pp. 317–35.

Alvesson, M., and Kärreman, D. (2000). Varieties of discourse: on the study of organizations through discourse analysis. *Human Relations* 53(9):1125–49.

Alvesson M., and Kärreman, D. (2011a). Decolonializing discourse: critical reflections on organizational discourse analysis. *Human Relations* 64(9): 1121–46.

Alvesson M., and Kärreman, D. (2011b). Organizational discourse analysis – well done or too rare? A reply to our critics. *Human Relations* 64(9): 1193–1202.

Aristotle (1992). *The Art of Rhetoric*. New York: Penguin.

Ashcraft, K. L. (2000). Empowering "professional" relationships: organizational communication meets feminist practice. *Management Communication Quarterly* 13: 347–92.

Ashcraft, K. L. (2004). Gender, discourse and organization: framing a shifting relationship. In D. Grant, C. Hardy, C. Oswick, and L. L. Putnam (eds), *The Sage Handbook of Organizational Discourse*. Thousand Oaks, CA: Sage, pp. 275–98.

Ashcraft, K. L. (2005). Feminist organizational communication studies: engaging gender in public and private. In S. May and D. K. Mumby (eds), *Engaging Organizational Communication Theory and Research: Multiple Perspectives*. Thousand Oaks, CA: Sage, pp. 141–70.

Ashcraft, K. L., Kuhn, T., and Cooren, F. (2009). Constitutional amendments:

References

"materializing" organizational communication. *The Academy of Management Annals* 3(1): 1–64.

Ashcraft, K. L., and Mumby, D. K. (2004). *Reworking Gender: A Feminist Communicology of Organization*. Thousand Oaks, CA: Sage.

Atkinson, J. M. and Heritage, J. (eds). (1984). *Structures of Social Action: Studies of Conversation Analysis*. Cambridge: Cambridge University Press, pp. 191–222.

Austin, J. L. (1962). *How To Do Things with Words*. Cambridge, MA: Harvard University Press.

Barge, J. K. (2004). Antenarrative and managerial practice. *Communication Studies* 55(1): 106–27.

Bargiela-Chiappini, F. (2011). Discourse(s), social construction and language practices. In conversation with Alvesson and Kärreman. *Human Relations* 64(9): 1177–91

Barker, J. R. (1993). Tightening the iron cage: concertive control in self-managing teams. *Administrative Science Quarterly* 38(3): 408–37.

Barker, J. R. (1999). *The Discipline of Teamwork: Participation and Concertive Control*. Thousand Oaks, CA: Sage.

Barthes, R. (1977). Introduction to the structural analysis of narratives. In *Image, Music, Text*. New York: Hill and Wang, pp. 32–51.

Barthes, R. (1988). *The Semiotic Challenge*, trans. R. Howard. New York: Hill and Wang.

Bencherki, N., and Cooren, F. (2011). Having to be: the possessive constitution of organization. *Human Relations* 64(12): 1579–1607.

Benoit-Barné, C. (2009). Reflections on science and technology controversies, material recalcitrance and empty reservoirs that suddenly become full. In S. Jacobs (ed.), *Concerning Argument: Selected Papers from the 15th Biennial Conference on Argumentation*. Washington, DC: National Communication Association, pp. 70–7.

Benoit-Barné, C., and Cooren, F. (2009). The accomplishment of authority through presentification: how authority is distributed among and negotiated by organizational members. *Management Communication Quarterly* 23(1): 5–31.

Benveniste, É. (1969). *Le vocabulaire des institutions indo-européennes* [*The vocabulary of Indo-European institutions*], vol. 2. Paris: Éditions de Minuit.

Bergström, O., and Knights, D. (2006). Organizational discourse and subjectivity: subjectification during processes of recruitment. *Human Relations* 59(3): 351–77.

Bhatia, A. (2006). Critical discourse analysis of political press conferences. *Discourse & Society* 17(2): 173–203.

Bitzer, L. F. (1968). The rhetorical situation. *Philosophy and Rhetoric* 1(1): 1–14.

Boden, D. (1994). *The Business of Talk: Organizations in Action*. Cambridge: Polity.

References

Boje, D. M. (1991). The storytelling organization: a study of story performance in an office-supply firm. *Administrative Science Quarterly* 36: 106–26.

Boje, D. M. (1995). Stories of the storytelling organization: a postmodern analysis of Disney as "Tamara-Land." *Academy of Management Journal* 38(4): 997–1035.

Bourdieu, P. (1991). *Language and Symbolic Power*, trans. G. R. M. Adamson. Cambridge: Polity.

Broadfoot, K., Deetz, S., and Anderson, D. (2004). Multi-levelled, multi-method approaches to organizational discourse. In D. Grant, C. Hardy, C. Oswick, and L. L. putnam (eds), *The Sage Handbook of Organizational Discourse*. Thousand Oaks, CA: Sage, pp. 193–211.

Browning, L. D., and Weick, K. E. (1986). Argument and narration in organizational communication. *Journal of Management* 12(2): 243–59.

Brummans, B. H. J. M., Cooren, F., and Chaput, M. (2009). Discourse, communication, and organisational ontology. In F. Bargiela-Chiappini (ed.), *The Handbook of Business Discourse*. Edinburgh: Edinburgh University Press, pp. 53–65.

Bruner, J. (1991). The narrative construction of reality. *Critical Inquiry* 18: 1–21.

Bruner, J. (2003). *Making Stories: Law, Literature, Life*. Cambridge, MA: Harvard University Press.

Buckley, W. (1967). *Sociology and Modern Systems Theory*. Englewood Cliffs, NJ: Prentice Hall.

Burke, K. (1945/1962). *A Grammar of Motives*. Berkeley, CA: University of California Press.

Burke, K. (1969). *A Rhetoric of Motives*. Berkeley/Los Angeles/London: University of California Press.

Chaput, M., Brummans, B. H. J. M., and Cooren, F. (2011). The role of organizational identification in the communicative constitution of an organization: a study of consubstantialization in a young political party. *Management Communication Quarterly* 25(2): 252–82.

Charland, M. (1987). Constitutive rhetoric: the case of the Peuple Québécois. *The Quarterly Journal of Speech* 73: 133–50.

Charland, M. (1990). Rehabilitating rhetoric: confronting blindspots in discourse and social theory. *Communication* 11: 253–64.

Cheney, G. (1983). The rhetoric of identification and the study of organizational communication. *Quarterly Journal of Speech* 69(2): 143–58.

Cheney, G. (1991). *Rhetoric in an Organizational Society: Managing Multiple Identities*. Columbia, SC: University of South Carolina Press.

Cheney, G. (1997). The many meanings of "solidarity." The negotiations of values in the Mondragón worker-cooperative complex under pressure. In B. D. Sypher (ed.), *Case Studies in Organizational Communication*, vol. 2. New York: Guilford, pp. 68–84.

171

References

Cheney, G. (1999). *Values at Work: Employees Participation Meets Market Pressure at Mondragón*. Ithaca, NY: Cornell University Press.

Cheney, G., and Christensen, L. T. (2001). Organizational identity: linkages between internal and external communication. In F. M. Jablin and L. L. Putnam (eds), *The New Handbook of Organizational Communication: Advances in Theory, Research, and Methods*. Thousand Oaks, CA: Sage, pp. 231–69.

Cheney, G., and Tompkins, P. (1987). Coming to terms with organizational identification and commitment. *Central States Speech Journal* 38(1): 1–15.

Cheney, G., Christensen, L. T., Conrad, C., and Lair, D. J. (2004). Corporate rhetoric as organizational discourse. In D. Grant, C. Hardy, C. Oswick, and L. L. Putnam (eds), *The Sage Handbook of Organizational Discourse*. London: Sage, pp. 79–103.

Chomsky, N. (1957). *Syntactic Structures*. The Hague, Netherlands: Mouton.

Chomsky, N. (1997). *The Minimalist Program*. Cambridge, MA: MIT Press.

Christensen, L. T., and Askegaard, S. (2001). Corporate identity and corporate image revisited: a semiotic perspective. *European Journal of Marketing* 35(3/4): 292–315.

Conrad, C. (1993). Rhetorical/communication theory as an ontology for structuration research. In *Communication Yearbook*, vol. 16. Newbury Park, CA: Sage, pp. 197–208.

Conrad, C. (2004). Organizational discourse: avoiding the determinism–voluntarism trap. *Organization* 11(3): 427–39.

Contractor, N. S., and Seibold, D. R. (1993). Theoretical frameworks for the study of structuring processes in group decision support systems: adaptive structuration theory and self-organizing systems theory. *Human Communication Research* 19: 528–63.

Cooren, F. (2000). *The Organizing Property of Communication*. Amsterdam/Philadelphia, PA: John Benjamins.

Cooren, F. (2001). Acting and organizing: how speech acts structure organizational interactions. *Concepts and Transformation* 6(3): 275–93.

Cooren, F. (2004). Textual agency: how texts do things in organizational settings. *Organization* 11(3): 373–93.

Cooren, F. (2006). The organizational world as a plenum of agencies. In F. Cooren, J. R. Taylor and E. J. Van Every (eds), *Communication as Organizing: Empirical and Theoretical Explorations in the Dynamic of Text and Conversation*. Mahwah, NJ: Lawrence Erlbaum, pp. 81–100.

Cooren, F. (2007). *Interacting and Organizing: Analyses of a Management Meeting*. Mahwah, NJ: Lawrence Erlbaum.

Cooren, F. (2008). Between semiotics and pragmatics: opening language studies to textual agency. *Journal of Pragmatics* 40: 1–16.

Cooren, F. (2010). *Action and Agency in Dialogue: Passion, Incarnation, and Ventriloquism*. Amsterdam/Philadelphia, PA: John Benjamins.

References

Cooren, F. (2012). Communication theory at the center: ventriloquism and the communicative constitution of reality. *Journal of Communication* 62: 1–20.

Cooren, F., and Bencherki, N. (2010). How things do things with words: ventriloquism, passion and technology. *Encyclopaideia* XIV(28): 35–62.

Cooren, F., and Fairhurst, G. T. (2004). Speech timing and spacing: the phenomenon of organizational closure. *Organization* 11(6): 793–824.

Cooren, F., and Matte, F. (2010). For a constitutive pragmatics: Obama, Médecins Sans Frontières and the measuring stick. *Pragmatics and Society* 1(1): 9–31.

Cooren, F., and Robichaud, D. (2010). Les approches constitutives [the constitutive approaches]. In S. Grosjean and L. Bonneville (eds), *Communication organisationnelle: approches, processus et enjeux [Organizational Communication: Approaches, Processes and Issues]*. Montreal, Canada: Gaëtan Morin.

Cooren, F., Taylor, J. R., and Van Every, E. J. (eds). (2006). *Communication as Organizing: Empirical and Theoretical Explorations in the Dynamic of Text and Conversation.* Mahwah, NJ: Lawrence Erlbaum.

Cooren, F., Bencherki, N., Chaput, M., and Vasquez, C. (forthcoming). Exploring fleeting moments of strategy: the communicative constitution of strategy-making. In D. Golsorkhi, L. Rouleau, D. Seidl, and E. Vaara (eds), *The Cambridge Handbook of Strategy as Practice.* Cambridge: Cambridge University Press.

Cooren, F., Brummans, B. H. J. M., Benoit-Barné, C., and Matte, F. (2013). A constituição comunicativa da cultura organizacional: uma questão a ser cultivada [The communicative constitution of organizational culture: a question of cultivation]. In M. Marchiori (ed.), *Faces da Cultura e da Comunicação Organizacional [Faces of Organizational Culture and Communication]*, vol. 3. Sao Caetano do Sul, Brazil: Difusao Editora, pp. 153–79.

Cooren, F., Matte, F., Vasquez, C., and Taylor, J. R. (2007). A humanitarian organization in action: organizational discourse as an immutable mobile. *Discourse and Communication* 1(2): 153–90.

Craig, R. T. (1999). Communication theory as a field. *Communication Theory* 9(2): 119–61.

Czarniawska, B. (1997a). A four times told tale: combining narrative and scientific knowledge in organization studies. *Organization* 4(1): 7–30.

Czarniawska, B. (1997b). *Narrating the Organization: Dramas of Institutional Identity.* Chicago/London: University of Chicago Press.

Czarniawska, B., and Gagliardi, P. (eds). (2003). *Narratives We Organize By.* Amsterdam, Netherlands: John Benjamins.

Deetz, S. (1992). *Democracy in an Age of Corporate Colonization: Developments in Communication and the Politics of Everyday Life.* Albany, NY: State University of New York Press.

Deetz, S. (2001). Conceptual foundations. In F. M. Jablin and L. L. Putnam (eds),

References

The New Handbook of Organizational Communication: Advances in Theory, Research, and Methods. Thousand Oaks, CA: Sage, pp. 3–46.

Deetz, S., Heath, R., and MacDonald, J. (2007). On talking to not make decisions: a critical analysis of organizational talk. In F. Cooren (ed.), *Interacting and Organizing: Analyses of a Management Meeting.* Mahwah, NJ: Lawrence Erlbaum, pp. 225–44.

Deleuze, G., and Guattari, F. (1987). *A Thousand Plateaus: Capitalism and Schizophrenia.* Minneapolis, MN: University of Minnesota Press.

Derrida, J. (1988). *Limited Inc.* Evanston, IL: Northwestern University Press.

Dewey, J. (1916). What pragmatism means by practical. In *Essays in Experimental Logic.* Chicago, IL: University of Chicago, pp. 303–29.

Eco, U. (1979). *A Theory of Semiotics.* Bloomington, IN: Indiana University Press.

Edwards, D. (2005). Discursive Psychology. In K. Fitch and R. E. Sanders (eds), *Handbook of Language and Social Interaction.* Mahwah, NJ: Erlbaum, pp. 257–73.

Eisenberg, E. M., and Riley, P. (2001). Organizational Culture. In F. Jablin and L. L. Putnam (eds), *The New Handbook of Organizational Communication: Advances in Theory, Research, and Methods.* Thousand Oaks, CA: Sage, pp. 291–322.

Fairclough, N. (1992). *Discourse and Social Change.* Cambridge: Polity.

Fairclough, N. (1993). Critical discourse analysis and the marketisation of public discourse: the universities. *Discourse & Society* 4(2): 133–68.

Fairclough, N. (1995). *Critical Discourse Analysis: The Critical Study of Language.* London: Longman.

Fairclough, N. (2005). Discourse analysis in organization studies: the case for critical realism. *Organization Studies* 26(6): 915–39.

Fairhurst, G. T. (2007). *Discursive Leadership: In Conversation with Leadership Psychology.* Thousand Oaks, CA: Sage.

Fairhurst, G. T., and Cooren, F. (2004). Organizational language in use: interaction analysis, conversation analysis, and speech act schematics. In D. Grant, C. Hardy, C. Oswick, N. Phillips, and L. Putnam (eds), *Handbook of Organizational Discourse.* London: Sage, pp. 131–52.

Fairhurst, G. T., and Cooren, F. (2009). Leadership as the hybrid production of presence(s). *Leadership* 5(4): 469–90.

Fairhurst, G. T., and Putnam, L. L. (2004). Organizations as discursive constructions. *Communication Theory* 14(1): 5–26.

Fairhurst, G. T., and Sarr, R. A. (1996). *The Art of Framing: Managing the Language of Leadership.* San Francisco, CA: Jossey-Bass Publishers.

Fairhurst, G.T., and Uhl-Bien, M. (2012). Organizational discourse analysis (ODA): examining leadership as a relational process. *Leadership Quarterly* 23: 1043–62.

References

Feldman, M. (2000). Organizational routines as a source of continuous change. *Organization Science* 11: 611–29.

Feldman, M., and Pentland, B. (2005). Organizational routines and the macro-actor. In B. Czarniawska and T. Hernes (eds), *Actor-network Theory and Organizing*. Malmö, Sweden: Liber and Copenhagen Business School Press, pp. 91–111.

Fisher, W. R. (1984). Narration as a human communication paradigm: the case of public moral argument. *Communication Monographs* 51(1): 1–23.

Fisher, W. R. (1985). The narrative paradigm: an elaboration. *Communication Monographs* 52(December): 347–67.

Fisher, W. R. (1989). Clarifying the narrative paradigm. *Communication Monographs* 56: 55–8.

Ford, J. D., and Ford, L. W. (1995). The role of conversations in producing intentional change in organizations. *Academy of Management Review* 20(3): 541–70.

Forester, J. (1992). Critical ethnography: on fieldwork in a Habermasian way. In M. Alvesson and H. Willmott (eds), *Critical Management Studies*. London: Sage, pp. 46–65.

Foss, S. K., Foss, K. A., and Trapp, R. (1985). *Contemporary Perspectives on Rhetoric*. Prospect Heights, IL: Waveland Press.

Foucault, M. (1977a). *Discipline and Punish: The Birth of the Prison*, trans. A. Sheridan. New York: Vintage Books.

Foucault, M. (1977b). *The Archaeology of Knowledge*. London: Tavistock.

Foucault, M. (1978). Politics and the study of discourse. *Ideology and Consciousness* 3: 7–26.

Foucault, M. (1981). The order of discourse. In R. Young (ed.), *Untyping the Text: A Post-structuralist Reader*. Boston, MA: Routledge & Kegan Paul, pp. 48–78.

Foucault, M. (1984). Truth and power. In P. Rabinow (ed.), *The Foucault Reader*. New York : Pantheon Books, pp. 51–75.

Foucault, M. (1970/1989). *The Order of Things: An Archeology of the Human Sciences*. New York: Routledge.

Fox, R., and Fox, J. (2004). *Organizational Discourse: A Language-Ideology-Power Perspective*: Westport, CT: Praeger.

Gabriel, Y. (1998). Same old story or changing stories? Folkloric, modern and postmodern mutations. In D. Grant, T. Keenoy, and C. Oswick (eds), *Discourse and Organization*. London: Sage, pp. 84–103.

Gabriel, Y. (2000). *Storytelling in Organizations: Facts, Fictions and Fantasies*. Oxford: Oxford University Press.

Gabriel, Y. (2004). Narratives, stories and texts. In D. Grant, C. Hardy, C. Oswick, and L. L. Putnam (eds), *The Sage Handbook of Organizational Discourse*. Thousand Oaks, CA: Sage, pp. 61–77.

References

Garfinkel, H. (1967). *Studies in Ethnomethodology*. Englewood Cliffs, NJ: Prentice Hall.

Garfinkel, H. (2002). *Ethnomethodology's Program: Working out Durkheim's Aphorism*. Lanham, MD: Rowman & Littlefield Publishers.

Gee, J. P. (1990). *Social Linguistics and Literacies: Ideology in Discourses*. New York: Routledge.

Gee, J. P. (1999). *An Introduction to Discourse Analysis: Theory and Method*. London: Routledge.

Geertz, C. (1973). *The Interpretation of Cultures: Selected Essays*. New York: Basic Books.

Gergen, K. J., Gergen, M. M., and Barrett, F. J. (2004). Dialogue: life and death of the organization. In D. Grant, C. Hardy, C. Oswick, and L. L. Putnam (eds), *The Sage Handbook of Organizational Discourse*. Thousand Oaks, CA: Sage, pp. 39–59.

Giddens, A. (1979). *Central Problems in Social Theory: Action, Structure and Contradiction in Social Analysis*. London: Macmillan.

Grant, D., Hardy, C., Oswick, C., Phillips, N., and Putnam, L. (eds). (2004). *Handbook of Organizational Discourse*. London: Sage.

Greimas, A. J. (1983). *Structural Semantics: An Attempt at a Method*. Lincoln/London: University of Nebraska Press.

Greimas, A. J. (1987). *On Meaning: Selected Writings in Semiotic Theory*. London: Frances Pinter.

Grint, K. (2000). *The Arts of Leadership*. Oxford: Oxford University Press.

Grint, K. (2005). Problems, problems, problems: the social construction of "leadership." *Human Relations* 58(11): 1467–94.

Habermas, J. (1984). *The Theory of Communicative Action. Reason and the Rationalization of Society*, trans. T. McCarthy, vol. 1. Boston, MA: Beacon Press.

Hall, E. T. (1966). *The Hidden Dimension*. Garden City, NY: Doubleday.

Hardy, C. (2001). Researching organizational discourse. *International Studies of Management & Organization* 31(3): 25–47.

Hardy, C., and Grant, D. (2012). Readers beware: provocation, problematization and … problems. *Human Relations* 65(5): 547–66.

Hardy, C., Grant, D., Keenoy, T., Oswick, C., and Phillips, N. (2004). Organizational discourse. *Organizational Studies* 25(1): *passim*.

Harris, Z. S. (1952). Discourse analysis: a sample text. *Language* 28(1): 1–30.

Hatch, M. J., and Schultz, M. (1997). Relations between organizational culture, identity and image. *European Journal of Marketing* 31(5/6): 356–65.

Heath, C., and Luff, P. (2000). *Technology in Action*. Cambridge: Cambridge University Press.

Heath, C., Luff, P., and Knoblauch, H. (2004). Tools, technologies and organizational interaction: the emergence of workplace studies. In D. Grant, C. Hardy,

References

C. Oswick, and L. Putman (eds), *The Sage Handbook of Organizational Discourse*. London: Sage, pp. 337–59.

Heath, R. L., Toth, E. L., and Waymer, D. (eds). (2009). *Rhetorical and Critical Approaches to Public Relations II*. New York: Routledge.

Heritage, J. (1984). *Garfinkel and Ethnomethodology*. Cambridge: Polity.

Hodge, R., and Kress, G. (1988). *Social Semiotics*. Cambridge: Polity.

Huspeck, M., and Kendall, K. E. (1991). On withholding political voice: an analysis of the political vocabulary of a "nonpolitical" speech community, *Quarterly Journal of Speech* 77(1): 1–19.

Hutchby, I., and Wooffitt, R. (2008). *Conversation Analysis*. Cambridge: Polity.

Iedema, R. (2001). Resemiotization. *Semiotica* 137(1–4): 23–39.

Iedema, R. (2003). Multimodality, resemiotization: extending the analysis of discourse as multi-semiotic practice. *Visual Communication* 2(1): 29–57.

Iedema, R. (2011). Discourse studies in the 21st century: a response to Mats Alvesson and Dan Kärreman's "decolonializing discourse." *Human Relations* 64(9): 1163–76.

Iedema, R., and Wodak, R. (1999), Introduction: organizational discourses and practices. *Discourse and Society* 10(1): 5–19.

Jaworski, A., and Coupland, N. (eds). (1999). *The Discourse Reader*. London: Routledge.

Jefferson, G. (1984). On stepwise transition from talk about a trouble to inappropriately next-positioned matters. In J. M. Atkinson and J. Heritage (eds), *Structures of Social Action: Studies of Conversation Analysis*. Cambridge: Cambridge University Press, pp. 191–222.

Jian, G., Schmisseur, A. M., and Fairhurst, G. T. (2008a). Organizational discourse and communication: the progeny of Proteus. *Discourse & Communication* 2(3): 299–320.

Jian, G., Schmisseur, A. M., and Fairhurst, G. T. (2008b). The debate about organizational discourse and communication: a rejoinder. *Discourse & Communication* 2(3): 353–5.

Kärreman, D., and Alvesson, M. (2008). The communicative constitution of what ? A response to Jian et al. *Discourse & Communication* 2(3): 321–5.

Katz, D., and Kahn, R. L. (1966). *The Social Psychology of Organizations*. New York, London, Sydney: John Wiley & Sons, Inc.

Keenoy, T., Oswick, C., and Grant, D. (1997). Organizational discourses: texts and context. *Organization* 4(2): 147–57.

Kilduff, M. (1993). Deconstructing organizations. *Academy of Management Review* 18(1): 13–31.

Kilduff, M., and Kelemen, M. (2004). Deconstructing discourse. In D. Grant, C. Hardy, C. Oswick, and L. L. Putnam (eds), *The Sage Handbook of Organizational Discourse*. Thousand Oaks, CA: Sage, pp. 259–72.

Knights, D. (2002). Writing organizational analysis into Foucault. *Organization* 9(4): 575–93.

References

Knights, D., and Willmott, H. (1989). Power and subjectivity at work: from degradation to subjugation in social relations. *Sociology* 23(4): 535–58.

Kuhn, T., and Burk, N. R. (2014). Spatial design as sociomaterial practice: a (dis) organizing perspective on communicative constitution. In F. Cooren, E. Vaara, A. Langley, and H. Tsoukas (eds), *Language and Communication at Work: Discourse, Narrativity, and Organizing*. Oxford: Oxford University Press, pp. 147–72.

Latour, B. (1987). *Science in Action: How to Follow Scientists and Engineers through Society*. Cambridge, MA: Harvard University Press.

Latour, B. (1996). On Interobjectivity. *Mind, Culture, and Activity* 3(4): 228–45.

Latour, B. (2005). *Reassembling the Social: An Introduction to Actor-Network Theory*. London: Oxford University Press.

Latour, B. (2013). *An Inquiry into Modes of Existence: An Anthropology of the Moderns*. Cambridge, MA: Harvard University Press.

Lave, J., and Wenger, E. (1991). *Situated Learning: Legitimate Peripheral Participation*. Cambridge: Cambridge University Press.

Lerner, G. (1992). Assisted storytelling: deploying shared knoweldge as a practical matter. *Qualitative Sociology* 15(3): 247–71.

Levinson, S. C. (1983). *Pragmatics*. Cambridge: Cambridge University Press.

Lévi-Strauss, C. (1963). *Structural Anthropology*, vol. 1, trans. C. J. B. G. Schoepf. New York: Basic Books.

Lévi-Strauss, C. (1973). *Structural Anthropology 2*, vol. 2. New York: Basic Books.

Livingston, E. (1987). *Making Sense of Ethnomethodology*. London/New York: Routledge & Kegan Paul.

Locke, J. (1959/1690). *An Essay Concerning Human Understanding*, vols 1 and 2. New York: Dover Publications.

Lorino, P. (2014). From speech acts to act speeches: collective activity, a discursive process speaking the language of habits. In F. Cooren, E. Vaara, A. Langley, and H. Tsoukas (eds), *Language and Communication at Work: Discourse, Narrativity, and Organizing*. Oxford: Oxford University Press, pp. 95–124.

Luff, P. J., Hindmarsh, J., and Heath, C. (eds.). (2000). *Workplace Studies: Recovering Work Practice and Informing System Design*. Cambridge: Cambridge University Press.

Luhmann, N. (1995). *Social Systems*. Stanford, CA: Stanford University Press.

McGee, M. C. (1975). In search of the "people": a rhetorical alternative. *The Quarterly Journal of Speech* 61: 235–49.

McPhee, R. D. (2004). Text, agency, and organization in the light of structuration theory. *Organization* 11(3): 355–71.

McPhee, R. D., and Iverson, J. (2009). The communicative constitution of organizations: a framework for explanation. In L. L. Putnam and A. M.

Nicotera (eds), *Building Theories of Organization: The Constitutive Role of Communication*. New York: Routledge, pp. 21–47.

McPhee, R. D., and Zaug, P. (2000). The communicative constitution of organizations: a framework for explanation. *The Electronic Journal of Communication/ La revue électronique de communication* 10(1/2): 1–16.

Manning, P. K. (1979). Metaphors of the field: varieties of organizational discourse. *Administrative Science Quaterly* 24: 660–71.

Manning, P. K. (1987). *Semiotics and Fieldwork*. Thousand Oaks, CA: Sage.

Martin, J. (1992). *Cultures in Organizations: Three Perspectives*. Oxford: Oxford University Press.

Martin, J. (2001). *Organizational Culture: Mapping the Terrain*. Thousand Oaks, CA: Sage.

Maturana, H. R. (1991). Science in daily life: the ontology of scientific explanations. In F. Steier (ed.), *Research and Reflexivity: Self-Reflexivity as Social Process*. Newbury Park, CA: Sage, pp. 30–52.

Meunier, D., and Vasquez, C. (2008). On shadowing the hybrid character of actions: a communicational approach. *Communication Methods and Measures* 2(3): 167–92.

Mintzberg, H. (1970). Structured observation as a method to study managerial work. *Journal of Management Studies* 7(1): 87–104.

Mintzberg, H. (1973). *The Nature of Managerial Work*. New York: Harper & Row.

Motion, J., and Weaver, C. K. (2005). A discourse perspective for critical relations research: life sciences network and the battle for truth. *Journal of Public Relations Research* 17(1): 49–67.

Mumby, D. K. (1988). *Communication and Power in Organizations: Discourse, Ideology, and Domination*. Norwood, NJ: Ablex.

Mumby, D. K. (1997). Modernism, postmodernism, and communication studies: a rereading of an ongoing debate. *Communication Theory* 7(1): 1–28.

Mumby, D. K. (2004). Discourse, power, and ideology: unpacking the critical approach. In D. Grant, C. Hardy, C. Oswick, N. Phillips, and L. Putnam (eds), *The Sage Handbook of Organizational Discourse*. London: Sage, pp. 237–58.

Mumby, D. K. (2005). Theorizing resistance in organization studies: a dialectical approach. *Management Communication Quarterly* 19(1): 19–44.

Mumby, D. K. (2011). What's cooking in organizational discourse studies? A response to Alvesson and Kärreman. *Human Relations* 64(9): 1147–61.

Mumby, D. K., and Clair, R. P. (1997) Organizational discourse. In T. A. Van Dijk (ed.), *Discourse as Social Interaction*. London: Sage, pp. 181–205.

Norris, S., and Jones, R. H. (eds). (2005). *Discourse in Action: Introducing Mediated Discourse*. New York: Routledge.

Nöth, W. (1995). *Handbook of Semiotics*. Bloomington, IN: Indiana University Press.

Orr, J. (1996). *Talking about Machines*. Ithaca, NY: ILR Press.

References

Oswick, C., Keenoy, T., and Grant, D. (1997). Managerial discourses: words speak louder than actions? *Journal of Applied Management Studies* 6(1): 5–12.

Oswick, C., Putnam, L. L., and Keenoy, T. (2004). Tropes, discourse and organizing. In D. Grant, C. Hardy, C. Oswick, and L. L. Putnam (eds), *The Sage Handbook of Organizational Discourse*. Thousand Oaks, CA: Sage, pp. 105–27.

Pearce, W. B. (1994). *Interpersonal Communication: Making Social Worlds*. New York: HarperCollins.

Pearce, W. B., and Cronen, V. (1980). *Communication, Action, and Meaning: The Creation of Social Realities*. New York: Praeger.

Pearce, W. B., and Pearce, K. A. (1998). Transcendent storytelling: abilities for systemic practitioners and their clients. *Human Systems* 9: 167–85.

Peirce, C. S. (1877). The fixation of belief. *Popular Science Monthly* 12 (November): 1–15.

Perelman, C., and Olbrechts-Tyteca, L. (1969). *The New Rhetoric: A Treatise on Argumentation*. Notre Dame, IN: University of Notre Dame Press.

Perelman, C. (1982). *The Realm of Rhetoric*. Notre Dame, IN: University of Notre Dame Press.

Perelman, C. (1984). The new rhetoric and the rhetoricians: remembrances and comments. *Quarterly Journal of Speech* 70(2): 188–96.

Phillips, N., Lawrence, T. B., and Hardy, C. (2004). Discourse and institutions. *Academy of Management Review* 29(4): 635–52.

Pomerantz, A., and Fehr, B. J. (1997). Conversation analysis: an approach to the study of social action as sense making practices. In T. A. Van Dijk (ed.), *Discourse as Social Interaction*. London: Sage, pp. 64–91.

Pomerantz, A., and Fehr, B. J. (2011). Conversation analysis: an approach to the analysis of social interaction. In T. A. Van Dijk (ed.), *Discourse Studies: A Multidisciplinary Introduction*. London: Sage, pp. 165–90.

Potter, J. (1996). *Representing Reality: Discourse, Rhetoric and Social Construction*. London: Sage.

Potter, J., and Wetherell, M. (1987). *Discourse and Social Psychology: Beyond Attitudes and Behaviour*. London: Sage.

Propp, V. J. (1968). *Morphology of the Folktale*, 2nd edn. Austin, TX: University of Texas Press.

Putnam, L. L. (2004). Discourse analysis: mucking around with negotiation data. *International Negotiation* 10(1): 17–32.

Putnam, L. L. (2008). Images of the communication–discourse relationship. *Discourse & Communication* 2(3): 339–45.

Putnam, L. L., and Nicotera, A. M. (eds). (2009). *The Communicative Constitution of Organization: Centering Organizational Communication*. New York: Routledge.

Putnam, L. L., Nicotera, A. M., and McPhee, R. D. (2009). Introduction: communication constitutes organization. In L. L. Putnam and A. M. Nicotera (eds),

References

Building Theories of Organization: The Constitutive Role of Communication. New York: Routledge, pp. 1–19.

Quinn, R. W., and Dutton, J. E. (2005). Coordination as energy-in-conversation. *Academy of Management Review* 30(1): 36–57.

Quinn, R. W., and Worline, M. C. (2008). Enabling courageous collective action: Conversations from United Airlines Flight 93. *Organization Science* 19(4): 497–516.

Reed, M. (2010). Is communication constitutive of organization? *Management Communication Quarterly* 24(1): 151–7.

Rice, R. E., and Cooper, S. D. (2010). *Organizations and Unusual Routines: A Systems Analysis of Dysfunctional Feedback Processes*. Cambridge, MA: Cambridge University Press.

Robichaud, D. (2001). Interaction as a text: a semiotic look at an organizing process. *American Journal of Semiotics* 17(1): 141–61.

Robichaud, D. (2002). Greimas' semiotics and the analysis of organizational action. In P. B. Anderson, R. J. Clarke, K. Liu, and R. K. Stamper (eds), *Coordination and Communication Using Signs: Studies in Organizational Semiotics*. Boston, MA: Kluwer Academic Publishers, pp. 129–49.

Robichaud, D. (2003). Narrative institutions we organize by: the case of a municipal administration. In B. Czarniawska and P. Gagliardi (eds), *Narratives We Organize By: Narrative Approaches in Organizational Studies*. Amsterdam: John Benjamins, pp. 37–53.

Robichaud, D. (2006). Steps toward a relational view of agency. In F. Cooren, J. R. Taylor, and E. J. Van Every (eds), *Communication as Organizing: Empirical and Theoretical Explorations in the Dynamic of Text and Conversation*. Mahwah, NJ: Lawrence Erlbaum Associates, pp. 101–14.

Robichaud, D., Giroux, H., and Taylor, J. R. (2004). The meta-conversation: the recursive property of language as the key to organizing. *Academy of Management Review* 29(4): 617–34.

Saussure, F. d. (1959). *Course in General Linguistics*, trans.W. Baskin, ed. Charles Bally and Albert Sechehaye. New York: Philosophical Library.

Schiffrin, D. (1994). *Approaches to Discourse*. Oxford: Blackwell.

Schoeneborn, D. (2011). Organization as communication: a Luhmannian perspective. *Management Communication Quarterly* 25(4): 663–89.

Scollon, R., and Scollon, S. W. (2003). *Discourse in Place: Language in the Material World*. London: Routledge.

Searle, J. R. (1969). *Speech Acts: An Essay in the Philosophy of Language*. London: Cambridge University Press.

Searle, J. R. (1979). *Expression and Meaning. Studies in the Theory of Speech Acts*. Cambridge: Cambridge University Press.

Shotter, J. (1984). *Social Accountability and Selfhood*. Oxford: Blackwell.

Shotter, J. (1993). *Conversational Realities: Constructing Life Through Language*. London: Sage.

References

Sigman, S. J. (1995). *The Consequentiality of Communication*. Hillsdale, NJ: Lawrence Erlbaum.

Silverman, D. (1998). *Harvey Sacks: Social Science and Conversation Analysis*. New York: Oxford University Press.

Smith, R., and Eisenberg, E. (1987). Conflict at Disneyland: a root metaphor analysis. *Communication Monographs* 54: 367–80.

Stubbs, M. (1983). *Discourse Analysis: The Sociolinguistic Analysis of Natural Language*. Oxford: Blackwell

Suchman, L. (1995). Making Work Visible. *Communications of the ACM* 38(9): 56–64.

Suchman, L. (2000). Organizing alignment: a case of bridge-building. *Organization* 7(2): 311–27.

Suchman, L. (2007). *Human-machine Reconfigurations: Plans and Situated Actions*. Cambridge: Cambridge University Press.

Tarde, G. (1895/2012). *Monadology and Sociology*. Melbourne, Australia: re.press.

Taylor, J. R. (1988). *Une organisation n'est qu'un tissu de communication* [*An Organization is Nothing but a Network of Communication*]. Montréal: Cahiers de recherches en communication.

Taylor, J. R. (1993). *Rethinking the Theory of Organizational Communication: How to Read an Organization*. Norwood, NJ: Ablex.

Taylor, J. R. (1995). Shifting from a heteronomous to an autonomous worldview of organizational communication: communication theory on the cusp. *Communication Theory* 5(1): 1–35.

Taylor, J. R. (2008). Communication and discourse: is the bridge language? Response to Jian et al. *Discourse & Communication* 2(3): 347–52.

Taylor, J. R., and Cooren, F. (1997). What makes communication "organizational"? How the many voices of a collectivity become the one voice of an organization. *Journal of Pragmatics* 27: 409–38.

Taylor, J. R., and Cooren, F. (2006). Making worldview sense: and paying homage, retrospectively, to Algirdas Greimas. In F. Cooren, J. R. Taylor, and E. J. Van Every (eds), *Communication as Organizing: Empirical and Theoretical Explorations in the Dynamic of Text and Conversation*. Mahwah, NJ: Lawrence Erlbaum, pp. 115–38.

Taylor, J. R., and Robichaud, D. (2007). Management as metaconversation: the search for closure. In F. Cooren (ed.), *Interacting and Organizing: Analyses of a Management Meeting*. Mahwah, NJ: Lawrence Erlbaum, pp. 5–30.

Taylor, J. R., and Van Every, E. J. (2000). *The Emergent Organization: Communication as Site and Surface*. Mahwah, NJ: Lawrence Erlbaum Associates.

Taylor, J. R., and Van Every, E. J. (2011). *The Situated Organization*. New York: Routledge.

References

Taylor, J. R., and Van Every, E. J. (2014). *When Organizations Fail: Why Authority Matters*. New York: Routledge.

Taylor, J. R., Cooren, F., Giroux, N., and Robichaud, D. (1996). The communicational basis of organization: between the conversation and the text. *Communication Theory* 6(1): 1–39.

Tompkins, P. K. (1993). *Organizational Communication Imperatives. Lessons of the Space Program*. Los Angeles, CA: Roxbury Publishing Company.

Tompkins, P. K., and Cheney, G. (1985). Communication and unobtrusive control in contemporary organizations. In R. D. McPhee and P. K. Tompkins (eds), *Organizational Communication: Traditional Themes and New Directions*. Beverly Hills, CA: Sage, pp. 179–210.

Vaara, E., and Tienari, J. (2002). Justification, legitimization and naturalization of mergers and acquisitions: a critical discourse analysis of media texts. *Organization* 9(2): 275–304.

Vaara, E., and Whittington, R. (2012). Strategy-as-practice: taking social practices seriously. *The Academy of Management Annals* 6(1): 285–336.

van Dijk, T. A. (1993). Principles of critical discourse analysis. *Discourse & Society* 4(2): 249–83.

van Dijk, T. A. (ed.). (1997a). *Discourse as Structure and Process*, vol. 1. London: Sage.

van Dijk, T. A. (ed.). (1997b). *Discourse as Social Interaction*, vol. 2. London: Sage.

Van Maanen, J. (2011). Ethnography as work: some rules of engagement. *Journal of Management Studies* 48(1): 218–34.

Vasquez, C. (2013). Spacing organization (or how to be here and there at the same time). In D. Robichaud and F. Cooren (eds), *Organization and Organizing: Materiality, Agency, and Discourse*. New York: Routledge, pp. 127–49.

Weick, K. E. (1979). *The Social Psychology of Organizing*. New York: Random House.

Weick, K. E. (1995). *Sensemaking in Organizations*. Thousand Oaks, CA: Sage.

Wenger, E., McDermott, R., and Snyder, W. M. (2002). *Cultivating Communities of Practice*. Cambridge, MA: Harvard Business Review Press.

Wetherell, M. (1998). Positioning and interpretative repertoires: conversation analysis and post-structuralism in dialogue. *Discourse & Society* 9: 387–412.

Whetten, D. A. (2006). Albert and Whetten revisited: strengthening the concept of organizational identity. *Journal of Management Inquiry* 15(3): 219–34.

Wikipedia (2014). Blind men and an elephant. *Wikipedia: The Free Encyclopedia*. FL: Wikimedia Foundation, Inc. From: <http://en.wikipedia.org/wiki/Blind_men_and_an_elephant>.

Witten, M. (1993). Narrative and the culture of obedience at the workplace. In D. K. Mumby (ed.), *Narrative and Social Control: Critical Perspectives*. Newbury Park, CA: Sage, pp. 97–118.

References

Wittgenstein, L. (1953). *Philosophical Investigations*. Oxford: Blackwell.

Wodak, R. (1999). Critical discourse analysis at the end of the 20th century. *Research on Language and Social Interaction* 32(1–2): 185–93.

Zachry, M. (2009). Rhetorical analysis. In F. Bargiela-Chiappini (ed.), *The Handbook of Business Discourse*. Edinburgh: Edinburgh University Press, pp. 68–79.

Index

185

Index

Index

Index

Index

Index